The media's watching Vault! Here's a sampling of our coverage.

"Lawyers looking for the scoop on the nation's biggest law firms now have a place to go."
– *The Wall Street Journal*

"With reviews and profiles of firms that one associate calls 'spot on', [Vault's] guide has become a key reference for those who want to know what it takes to get hired by a law firm and what to expect once they get there."
– *New York Law Journal*

"The best place on the web to prepare for a job search."
– *Fortune*

"Vault is indispensable for locating insider information."
– *Metropolitan Corporate Counsel*

"[Vault's guide] is an INVALUABLE Cliff's Notes to prepare for interviews."
– *Women's Lawyer's Journal*

"For those hoping to climb the ladder of success, [Vault's] insights are priceless."
– *Money Magazine*

"[Vault guides] make for excellent starting points for job hunters and should be purchased by academic libraries for their career sections [and] university career centers."
– *Library Journal*

SIMPSON THACHER

The Tax Practice

The tax practice at Simpson Thacher is dedicated to solving complex transactional and financial problems for a diverse group of clients, including major multinational corporations, investment and commercial banks, merchant banking funds and wealthy individuals. While the practice encompasses a broad range of matters, our principal focus is on the tax aspects of merger and acquisition transactions, the design of complex financial instruments, the formation of investment funds and other capital pools, the structuring of real estate investments, and cross-border financing and investment activity.

For more information about the Firm, please contact Dee Pifer, Director of Legal Employment, at: dpifer@stblaw.com

NEW YORK
425 Lexington Ave.
New York, NY 10017
Tel: (212) 455-2500

LOS ANGELES
1999 Ave. of the Stars
Los Angeles, CA 90067
Tel: (310) 407-7500

PALO ALTO
3330 Hillview Avenue
Palo Alto, CA 94304
Tel: (650) 251-5000

HONG KONG
Asia Pacific Finance Tower
3 Garden Road
Central Hong Kong
Tel: 852-2514-7600

LONDON
CityPoint
One Ropemaker Street
London EC2Y 9HU
United Kingdom
Tel: 44-20-7275-6500

TOKYO
Ark Mori Building
1-Chome-12-32, Akasaka
Minato-Ku,
Tokyo 107-6030
Tel: 81-3-5562-8601

www.simpsonthacher.com
SIMPSON THACHER & BARTLETT LLP

VAULT GUIDE TO TAX LAW CAREERS

© 2004 Vault Inc.

VAULT GUIDE TO TAX LAW CAREERS

WRITTEN BY SHANNON KING NASH
EDITED BY VERA DJORDJEVICH
AND THE STAFF OF VAULT

© 2004 Vault Inc.

Copyright © 2004 by Vault Inc. All rights reserved.

All information in this book is subject to change without notice. Vault makes no claims as to the accuracy and reliability of the information contained within and disclaims all warranties. No part of this book may be reproduced or transmitted in any form or by any means, electronic or mechanical, for any purpose, without the express written permission of Vault Inc.

Vault, the Vault logo, and "the most trusted name in career information™" are trademarks of Vault Inc.

For information about permission to reproduce selections from this book, contact Vault Inc., 150 W. 22nd St., 5th Floor, New York, NY 10011, (212) 366-4212.

Library of Congress Cataloging-in-Publication Data

Nash, Shannon King.
   Vault guide to tax law careers / Shannon King Nash ; edited by Vera Djordjevich and the staff of Vault.
      p. cm.
  ISBN 1-58131-273-3 (alk. paper)
 1. Tax lawyers--United States. 2. Law--Vocational guidance--United States. I. Title: Tax law careers. II. Djordjevich, Vera. III. Vault (Firm) IV. Title.
  KF299.T3N37 2004
  343.7304'023--dc22

                                                                                                          2004009751

Printed in the United States of America

ACKNOWLEDGMENTS

Shannon King Nash's acknowledgments: I would like to thank my loving family, Bill, Jason and Kyle. Thanks for all of your undying support and confidence in me. I would also like to thank all of my friends and colleagues who served as my inspiration for this guide and shared so many of their personal stories, successes and failures. In particular I would like to thank my dear friend Wayne Hamilton for his words of wisdom, suggestions and for reading every last word, sometimes more than once.

Vault's acknowledgments: Thanks to everyone who had a hand in making this book possible, especially Marcy Lerner, Ed Shen, Kelly Shore, Tyya Turner and Elena Boldeskou. We are also extremely grateful to Vault's entire staff for all their help in the editorial, production and marketing processes. Vault also would like to acknowledge the support of our investors, clients, employees, family, and friends. Thank you!

McDermott Will & Emery

15 offices worldwide

40 practice and industry areas

1000 lawyers

...and endless opportunities.

Join us.

McDermott Will & Emery

Lydia Kelley, Hiring Partner
227 West Monroe Street
Chicago, Illinois 60606-5096
312.984.6470
lkelley@mwe.com
www.mwe.com

Boston Brussels Chicago Düsseldorf London
Los Angeles Miami Milan Munich New York
Orange County Rome San Diego Silicon Valley
Washington, D.C.

Table of Contents

THE SCOOP 1

The Tax Law Industry 3
A Brief History of Federal Tax Laws 4
Sources of Tax Law 7
The Internal Revenue Service 11
The Courts 16
Key Tax Doctrines 18

Tax Lawyers in All Shapes and Sizes 23
Who They Are 23
Tax Specialties 26
Where They Work 33

Taxing Trends 37
Jobs, Jobs and More Jobs 37
Flat Tax, National Sales Tax, Value-Added Tax, No Tax 39
Is it Really All Good? 40

ON THE JOB 45

Job Responsibilities 47
Research 47
Writing 48
Billing 50

Tax Law Employers 51
Law Firms 51
Accounting Firms 59
Corporations 64
Government 67
Academia 74

Employer FAQs   77

Your First Tax Position 77
Making the Switch 78
Working Moms 85
Tax Law as a Second Career 86
Diversity Issues 86
Pro Bono Opportunities 87

A Day in the Life   91

Tax Associate, Employee Benefits at a Large East Coast Law Firm 91
Tax Associate, Corporate/Transactional Tax at
a Large Southern Law Firm 92
Tax Associate, Corporate Tax at a Large New York Law Firm 93
Tax Partner, Corporate Tax at a Large West Coast Law Firm 94
Solo Practitioner, General Tax Practice on the East Coast 95
Tax Planning and Controversy Attorney (In-House),
Privately-Held Large Corporation 96
Tax Planning Attorney (In-House), Focusing on State and Local Tax,
Fortune 500 Corporation in the Midwest 97
Tax Controversy Attorney (In-House),
Fortune 500 Corporation in the South 98
Tax Partner Focusing on Financial Institutions and Products,
Big Four Accounting Firms 99
Tax Manager Focusing on Estate Planning,
Big Four Accounting Firms 100
IRS Tax Attorney Practicing in Partnership Tax 101

GETTING HIRED   107

Education   109

Different Educational Paths 109
Accounting Background 111
Master's Degree in Taxation 112
Tax Classes in Law School 113
The LL.M Debate 114
Continuing Education 118

Hiring Process — 121

On-Campus Recruiting 121
Headhunters 122
Job Boards 123
Mass Mailing 123
Job Fairs 124
Increasing Your Marketability 125
Networking 128
Interview Tips 130

Cover Letters, Resumes and Addenda — 133

The Cover Letter 133
Your Resume 134
The Addendum 135
Sample Cover Letters, Resumes and Addenda 136

APPENDIX — 149

Top Tax Law Firms 152
Industry Organizations and Resources 153
Federal Agencies and Courts 158
Tax Research and News Services 159

About the Author — 163

THE SCOOP

Chapter 1: The Tax Law Industry

Chapter 2: Tax Lawyers in All Shapes and Sizes

Chapter 3: Taxing Trends

The Tax Law Industry

CHAPTER 1

We pay taxes in almost every part of our life – sales taxes on our food and clothing, airport taxes on our travel and even local taxes to attend a concert or event. But perhaps the most well-known tax, familiar to Americans from the time they're old enough to say "April 15", is the federal income tax.

The first federal income tax was enacted as part of the Revenue Act of 1862 and levied to finance the Civil War. It was followed by the Revenue Act of 1913, which serves as the basis for today's Internal Revenue Code. But the 1913 Tax Code was a mere 14 pages long. Since that time there have been many modifications and expansions, including some of the laws' most sweeping changes in 1954 and 1986. In fact, significant changes to the Tax Code now occur almost on an annual basis – not to mention all of the Treasury regulations and IRS rulings and pronouncements that are also changed or added. All in all, federal tax rules are contained in some 45,662 pages, or nearly 6,929,000 words, as estimated by the Tax Foundation.

The complex and ever-changing nature of tax law has spawned an entire industry for professionals who have mastered it. A University of Michigan study puts the cost of enforcing and complying with federal income taxes at around $115 billion per year. In a 2001 issue of <u>Policy Analysis</u>, published by the Cato Institute, Chris Edwards, the institute's director of fiscal policy studies, estimates that of the more than one million attorneys in the United States, some 10 percent practice in tax law.

For insight into the tax law industry, you must understand that it all starts with the Internal Revenue Code (the "Code" or the "Tax Code"). In addition, there are tax regulations that impact the Code and key tax doctrines that have evolved from court cases and legislation interpreting or modifying the Code. This chapter provides an overview of

- The history of the federal tax laws
- The Internal Revenue Code
- Tax legislation
- The Treasury Department and Treasury regulations
- The IRS and its rulings and other pronouncements
- The courts
- Key tax doctrines and concepts

A Brief History of Federal Tax Laws

This country has been dealing with taxes since the American colonies fought against the British. In order to pay for its wars with the French, the English Parliament imposed severe taxes on the American colonies, including the 1765 Stamp Act and the infamous tax on tea. The American Revolution, as every schoolchild learns, was fought around the rallying cry, "Taxation without representation is tyranny."

The first American income tax

From the beginning of the U.S. government, taxes, mostly in the form of tariffs, excises and sales taxes on consumer products (like tea, watches and gold), were imposed. The year 1862 marks the first time that an income tax was imposed; it was an emergency wartime measure to raise revenue during the Civil War. This 3 percent tax generally applied to those who earned more than $600. The revenues raised from these taxes were critical in financing the Union Army in the Civil War.

The first income tax was in effect for 10 years. It was repealed in 1872. Once the war had ended there was less justification for an income tax. Efforts to impose another federal income tax were thwarted when the U.S. Supreme Court declared the income tax unconstitutional in 1895. Under the Constitution, Congress could impose direct taxes only in proportion to a state's population. However, all of this changed in 1913.

The 16th Amendment and the Revenue Act of 1913

Both at home and abroad, 1913 was an eventful year. Woodrow Wilson became the 28th U.S. president. New York's Grand Central Station opened as the world's largest train station. The first Charlie Chaplin movies were made. Bulgaria's defeat by Greece, Serbia, Romania and Turkey in the Second Balkan War foreshadowed the start of World War I. 1913 also saw the births of civil rights leader Rosa Parks, former President Richard Nixon, labor leader Jimmy Hoffa, football legend Vince Lombardi, Olympic track and field star Jesse Owens and actors Burt Lancaster and Vivian Leigh was also born that year. The dollar went a long way by today's standards. Using the consumer price index, a dollar in 1913 would be worth $18.59 in 2003. It must have seemed to legislators like a good time to impose a new tax system.

In February 1913 the 16th Amendment to the U.S. Constitution was ratified. Amending Article I, Section 9, to allow the federal government to collect income taxes, the 16th amendment provides:

The Congress shall have power to lay and collect taxes on incomes, from whatever source derived, without apportionment among the several states, and without regard to any census or enumeration.

The first legislation imposing a federal income tax after the passage of the 16th Amendment was the Revenue Act of 1913. The law introduced Form 1040 as the standard tax reporting form and is the basis for today's Internal Revenue Code. Here are some other interesting highlights of the 1913 Act:

- The lowest tax rate of 1 percent applied to those with an annual income of $20,000.

- Taxpayers with incomes of over $500,000 paid tax at the rate of 6 percent.

- Less than 1 percent of the American population actually had to pay this income tax.

- The 1913 Tax Code was just 14 pages long.

- The actual tax return was only two pages long, with another page of instructions.

- Tax returns were due on March 1 and had to be signed under oath and in front of a magistrate or a justice of the peace.

- Some 350,000 tax returns were filed for 1913 – a number so small that the IRS had the resources to audit every return.

Tax withholding, the IRS and ERISA

The next major tax law change occurred in 1943, once again during wartime and introduced a development that has become a way of life for anyone with a job. Remember that feeling from your first summer job at the local ice cream parlor? You made $4 an hour, worked five days a week and eight hours a day. You finally received your first two-week paycheck. You opened the envelope, expecting a nice, fat check for $320, only to discover that someone had taken a chunk out, leaving you with just $300. Did your boss make a mistake? Unfortunately not. Welcome to the wonderful world of payroll tax withholding.

The federal payroll withholding tax system began in 1943 as part of the effort to raise more money for World War II. Payroll taxes include Social Security and Medicare taxes. Also known as the pay-as-you-go system, this system allows the government to collect money from taxpayers throughout the year instead of in lump-sum payments when tax returns are actually filed. This system was important in 1943 because money was sorely needed to finance the war effort. According to the Internal Revenue Service, approximately 90 percent of all American workers paid these taxes by the end of the war.

The 1950s brought about further developments of the federal tax system. In 1953, the Internal Revenue Service was established. The next year the Internal Revenue Act of 1954 was adopted, which significantly expanded the tax laws and served as the main tax act for many years. More reforms and refinements followed over the next two decades. The Tax Reform Act of 1969 changed the way that taxes were paid by Americans across socio-economic levels. High-income taxpayers and corporations were now required to pay higher rates of taxes while low-income taxpayers received increased deduction and exemptions to lower their tax burden.

Yet another important change in tax history was introduced in 1974. That year Congress enacted the Employee Retirement Income Security Act, or ERISA. ERISA provides the federal minimum standards for most pensions and health plans – thus spawning an entire sub-industry of tax lawyers who deal with pension plans and employee benefits.

Recent tax reform

By the 1980s, tax reform had become very popular. Despite efforts to establish a federal system that taxed people based on income levels, the wealthy had found many loopholes in what was now a very complicated Tax Code, and the system once again needed tweaking. The most sweeping changes made to the Code in recent history were made in 1986. The 1986 Federal Tax Reform Act was meant to pump money back into the economy by simplifying the overall tax law structure. Taxes were cut for the wealthy in the hope that they would stop trying to use loopholes and tax shelters and instead spend their tax savings. This law, which contained over 300 provisions and 2,700 revisions, serves as the basis for our current Tax Code. Many tax lawyers refer to a section of the Code as "Section X of the Internal Revenue Code of 1986, as amended."

Recent years have brought more tax law changes. In 2001, Congress passed the Economic Growth and Tax Relief Reconciliation Act. This was a major tax law, promising over one trillion dollars in tax reduction to be spread out until 2010. It made some 400 changes to the Code and was the most extensive tax law change since the 1980s. Two years later, the Jobs and Growth Tax Relief Reconciliation Act of 2003 came along. The 2003 law is the third-largest tax act in U.S. history and contains a smorgasbord of new tax rules, phases-ins and phase-outs, and tax benefits.

Today's Tax Code sports over 6 million words and is reflected in some 1,101 IRS publications, forms and instructions. Given the magnitude of the recent tax law changes, the future will likely hold more reform, more complexity and an even longer Code.

Sources of Tax Law

The Internal Revenue Code

All federal laws are codified in the United States Code. The Tax Code can be found in Title 26 of the U.S. Code. It started as just a few code sections and, according to the Tax Foundation, by 2000 covered over 725 U.S. Code sections.

The Tax Code is divided and subdivided into several levels and parts, including subtitles, chapters, subchapters, parts, subparts, sections and subsections. The subtitles of the Internal Revenue Code are grouped by various tax provisions identified by capital letters. Within each subtitle, there are individual chapters. Chapters are further divided into subchapters. Subchapters are split into parts, which may be further divided into subparts until we finally arrive at a particular Code section. Most references to the Tax Code are actually made to a particular Code section. But, of course, the complexity does not end there. Sections can be further divided into subsections, paragraphs, subparagraphs and clauses. For example, Section 707(a)(2)(A)(i) is broken down as:

- Section 707
- Subsection a
- Paragraph 2
- Subparagraph A
- Clause i

Tax legislation

It's evident that tax laws are not static but continue to grow, change and evolve – keeping tax attorneys busily employed. Tax legislation passed annually by Congress ensures the continued complexity of the Code.

Almost all tax legislation begins as a bill in the U.S. House of Representatives and, in particular, the House Ways and Means Committee. Once passed by this committee, the bill goes to the full House of Representatives for its approval. Changes are made and concessions are reached before the bill is finally sent to the Senate – usually landing in front of the Senate Finance Committee. Once through the Finance Committee, the bill is put before the entire Senate for approval. There are generally differences between the House and Senate versions of the bill so it is then sent to a Joint Conference Committee. When a compromise is finally reached, the new and improved bill is put in front of both houses of Congress. Once approved it is forwarded to the president for approval and, if signed by the president, the bill becomes law and thereby enters into the U.S. Tax Code.

An excellent way to determine why a section was added, changed or modified is to review the legislative history. Legislative histories can be found at the end of a bill; you can retrieve them through search services like LexisNexis and Westlaw. Legislative histories include reports from the House Ways and Means Committee, the Senate Finance Committee and the Joint Conference Committee, as well as hearings, debates, presidential messages and earlier drafts of the bill.

Federal tax legislation is enacted every year. Many changes are minor additions, corrections or modifications to the Code which fly completely under the radar screen for the average American. But in recent years, tax legislation has been at the forefront of many presidential and congressional platforms and these tax changes are frequently covered by the national media. For example, President Bush's 2003 tax package, which was finally passed in the Jobs and Growth Tax Relief Reconciliation Act of 2003, received just as much news coverage as whether or not J-Lo (Jennifer Lopez) and Ben Affleck, affectionately called Benifer, were still on track for their impending nuptials. (Since the couple abandoned their marriage plans in September, while President Bush's package made it into law, it seems that the president had better luck than the tender twosome.)

Treasury regulations

Once tax laws are enacted and become apart of the Internal Revenue Code they are administered and interpreted by two important government agencies: the U.S. Treasury Department and the Internal Revenue Service.

The Treasury Department has an Office of Tax Policy that helps the secretary of the treasury with tax-related matters such as developing and implementing federal tax policies and programs; providing estimates of all government receipts for the president's budget, fiscal policy decisions and Treasury cash management decisions; establishing policy criteria reflected in regulations and rulings; negotiating tax treaties for the United States and representing the United States in meetings of multilateral organizations dealing with tax policy matters; and providing economic and legal policy analysis for domestic and international tax policy decisions.

This section focuses on the Office of Tax Policy's role in establishing Treasury regulations. These regulations provide more detail as to how specific provisions of the Code work. You might compare the Internal Revenue Code to the abbreviated Cliff Notes version and the Treasury regulations to the detailed 700-page novel. For example, Section 501(c)(3) of the Internal Revenue Code covers tax-exempt organizations. It is approximately 133 words long and states:

Corporations, and any community chest, fund, or foundation, organized and operated exclusively for religious, charitable, scientific, testing for public safety, literary, or educational purposes, or to foster national or international amateur sports competition (but only if no part of its activities involve the provision of athletic facilities or equipment), or for the prevention of cruelty to children or animals, no part of the net earnings of which inures to the benefit of any private shareholder or individual, no substantial part of the activities of which is carrying on propaganda, or otherwise attempting, to influence legislation (except as otherwise provided in subsection (h)), and which does not participate in, or intervene in (including the publishing or distributing of statements), any political campaign on behalf of (or in opposition to) any candidate for public office.

This is the main section of the Code that discusses charitable organizations. According to the New Nonprofit Almanac and Desk References, a publication produced by the Independent Sector and the Urban Institute, there are some 1.2 million nonprofit organizations, employing almost 11 million people and accounting for about 6 percent of United State's annual income. Not a small industry. Yet the tax law that grants the prized tax-exempt status is only 133 words long. Certainly there must be more regulation of these entities. The answer, of course, can be found in the Treasury regulations. The Treasury regulations under 501(c)(3) go on for page after page and provide details on myriad tax issues affecting these organizations such as how to qualify as a tax-exempt organization, which private benefits to individuals or organizations are not permitted and what qualifies as income that may be subject to taxation (called unrelated business taxable income).

Treasury regulations fall into three categories – legislative, procedural and interpretative. Legislative regulations are issued when Congress enacts a statute specifically authorizing and directing the Treasury Department to issue such regulations. These regulations are not very common. However, they carry the full weight of good legal precedent and are not often overturned by courts. As its name suggests, procedural regulations cover procedural tax issues, such as how to file a private letter ruling request. These regulations may be overturned and are generally considered discretionary. Finally, interpretative regulations provide the Treasury's position on how a section should be administered or applied. Interpretative regulations are by far the most common (for example, the regulations discussed above for 501(c)(3) organizations are interpretive regulations). Unlike legislative regulations, interpretative regulations are often the subject of dispute and have been frequently overturned by the courts.

The Office of Tax Policy and the Internal Revenue Service work jointly on formulating and issuing Treasury regulations. Treasury regulations are usually drafted by the commissioner of the IRS and approved by the secretary of the treasury (through the Office of Tax Policy). These regulations often come into play after new tax laws are enacted or to clarify issues within existing tax laws.

Regulations are typically first issued in proposed form and published in the Federal Register – an official publication of rules, proposed rules and regulations of federal agencies and organizations including the IRS. Then, during a comment period, Treasury and the IRS solicit written comments from the public. Sometimes an oral hearing is held where taxpayers can present their comments on the proposed regulations. It can take months or even years for proposed regulations to be finalized. Although during this waiting period the proposed regulations are not binding on courts, they generally provide a good overview as to the IRS's position on a tax law issue. Taxpayers often use proposed regulations in planning and developing their tax positions.

Sometimes temporary regulations are issued – typically because the IRS has changed its interpretation of a section. These temporary regulations are effective upon publication and expire three years after their issuance. Proposed regulations are also usually issued simultaneously with temporary regulations. When the proposed or temporary regulations are finalized, they are issued as Treasury decisions and published in Title 26 of the Code of Federal Regulations.

The Internal Revenue Service

Overview

The Internal Revenue Service's roots can be traced as far back as 1862 when President Lincoln and Congress first established a commissioner of internal revenue. That position disappeared when the income tax act was repealed in 1872. The current agency's history goes back to 1952, as the primary government agency responsible for collecting federal taxes. At that time it was called the Bureau of Internal Revenue. The IRS is led by a commissioner and a chief counsel, both of whom are selected by the president and confirmed by the Senate. Although the secretary of the Treasury Department has the authority to administer federal tax laws, much of this authority has been delegated to the IRS. Thus, the IRS's primary role is to administer the tax laws and collect taxes. It does this by checking tax returns, collecting tax payments and issuing refunds to taxpayers.

The IRS collects some $1.7 trillion in tax revenues. According to the 1998 IRS Data Book, the IRS employs some 97,000 people and takes on over 74,000 volunteers during the tax filing season. Under the current IRS organizational chart, the IRS is led by a commissioner, who is selected by the president and confirmed by the Senate. The agency is divided into the following units:

Operating Divisions

Wage & Investment (W&I), which serves approximately 116 million taxpayers who file individual and joint tax returns.

Small Business & Self-Employed (SB/SE), which serves approximately 45 million small businesses and self-employed taxpayers.

Large & Mid-Size Business (LMSB), which serves corporations with assets of more than $10 million.

Tax Exempt & Government Entities (TE/GE), which serves employee benefit plans and tax-exempt organizations such as nonprofit charities and governmental entities.

Functional Units

Appeals, which serves as the alternative dispute resolution forum for taxpayers contesting an IRS compliance action. Appeals is an independent channel for taxpayers who have disputes with the IRS and the last opportunity for the IRS and the taxpayer to resolve controversies before going to litigation.

Criminal Investigation (CI), which investigates criminal violation of tax, money laundering and Bank Secrecy Act laws.

Taxpayer Advocate Services, which is an independent organization within the IRS that helps taxpayers resolve problems with the IRS and recommends changes to prevent such problems.

Shared Services

- *Information Systems Services*
- *Agency Capture Services*

Office of Chief Counsel

This office provides legal interpretations of the internal revenue laws, represents the IRS in litigation and provides overall legal support to the IRS. The office is led by the chief counsel, the highest-ranking legal office at the IRS. Like the commissioner, the chief counsel is selected by the president, subject to Senate confirmation. Next, there is a deputy chief counsel (technical) who oversees a group of lawyers divided by their expertise in substantive tax law areas and based on related Tax Code sections. A deputy chief counsel (operations) oversees senior legal executives who serve as division counsel for each operating division and provides legal advice and representation to operating division management. Examples of work performed by Chief Counsel lawyers include helping draft Treasury regulations, IRS rulings and other IRS-published guidance, representing the IRS before the Tax Court and providing specific legal advice and determinations to taxpayers on various IRS functions, both before and after tax returns are filed.

National Office Staff

- *Human Resources*
- *Finance*
- *Communication*

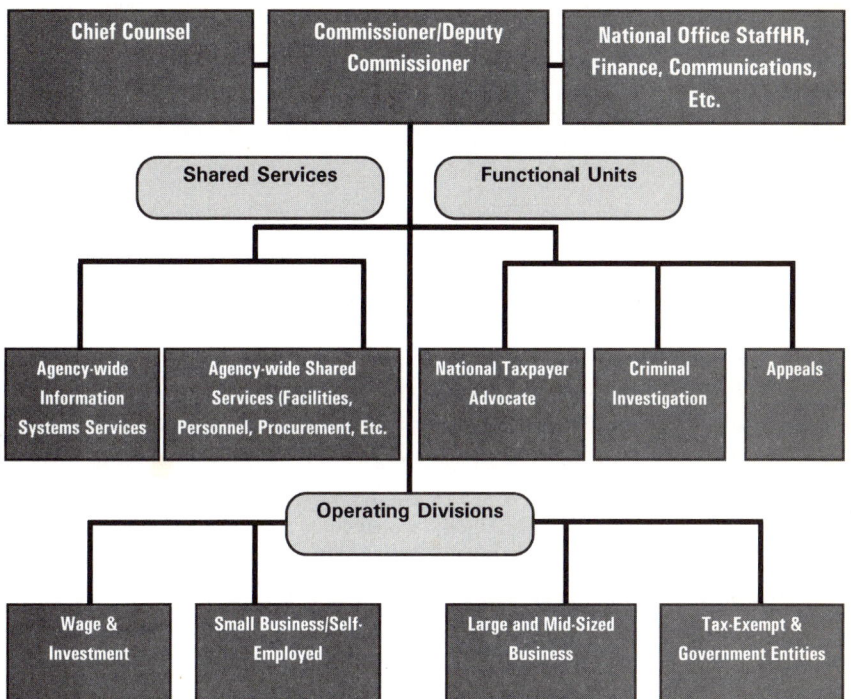

Rulings, pronouncements and publications

The IRS uses many different forms of guidance to provide its position on a particular tax matter. The following is a brief overview of some of these forms. Please note that is not an exhaustive list. Many of these documents may be downloaded from the IRS's web site at www.irs.gov. Others may be retrieved from search services like LexisNexis and Westlaw.

Revenue rulings

Revenue rulings provide the IRS's position with respect to a particular issue based on a specific set of facts. They are the highest form of IRS ruling in that taxpayers may rely on them in determining the tax consequences of their own transactions – hence they may serve as precedent. They are issued by the IRS National Office in Washington, D.C. They do not carry the same weight with the courts as Treasury regulations but are viewed merely as the agency's official position.

Revenue procedures

Revenue procedures outline the rights and duties of taxpayers under the Tax Code. They do not cover substantive laws like Treasury regulations or revenue rulings. They are also issued by the IRS National Office and may be cited as precedent.

Private letter rulings

Private letter rulings, or PLRs as they are commonly called, are issued by the IRS in response to requests by taxpayers. These rulings are written memoranda that explain how the IRS will treat a proposed transaction for taxpayers. The taxpayer requesting the ruling must submit a summary of the facts, the issue and the tax treatment he is seeking, along with a payment known as a user fee. These rulings, issued by the IRS National Office, are made public 90 days after they are issued to the taxpayer who requested the ruling. Private letter rulings are not generally considered to be precedent. Instead, they specifically apply only to the taxpayer who requested the ruling. They do, however, provide good guidance as to how the IRS will view a particular issue and are therefore often relied on by other taxpayers with similar fact patterns and issues.

Determination letters

Determination letters are very similar to private letter rulings. They are written memoranda, but they are issued by a local IRS district director, rather than the national office, in response to a taxpayer's request.

Technical advice memoranda

Technical advice memoranda (TAMs) are written memoranda furnished by the IRS National Office upon request by an IRS field agent. They are issued in response to a specific request for technical assistance with a particular issue that has arisen during the course of an audit or a matter in the appeals division. Appeals serves as an arbitrator between the taxpayer and the IRS field or examination agent who is auditing the taxpayer. These memoranda only apply to the taxpayers whose audit or appeals matter is being discussed. Allen Madison, a tax attorney with Fenwick & West LLP, explains that TAMs represent "the first opportunity for a taxpayer to win his or her case in audit before litigating the matter in court – like the first bite at the apple."

Technical memoranda

Technical memoranda, not to be confused with technical advice memoranda or TAMs, are written documents that explain the IRS's rationale behind Treasury decisions. These documents generally provide background information on Treasury regulations and are typically prepared by the IRS National Office in Washington, D.C.

Field service advice memoranda

Field service advice memoranda, or FSAs, are written advice or instructions prepared by the Office of Chief Counsel and issued to field or service center employees of the IRS. Like TAMs, field service memoranda are taxpayer-specific and cannot be used or cited as precedent.

General counsel memoranda

General counsel memoranda, or GCMs, are prepared by the IRS National Office in response to formal requests for legal advice from the IRS assistant commissioner. Generally, GCMs cover advice on proposed revenue rulings, technical advice memorandum and private letter rulings.

Actions on decisions

Actions on decisions (AODs) are legal memoranda prepared by the Office of Chief Counsel (Tax Litigation Division) after the IRS has lost a tax case. They explain whether the IRS agrees with the decision (called acquiescence) and why or, if the IRS disagrees with the decision, its non-acquiescence. An action on decision recommends the action that IRS personnel should take on tax issues similar to those in the underlying court decision.

Information releases

Information releases, typically issued by the IRS National Office, discuss matters of important public concern without applying these matters to a specific taxpayer or set of facts.

Publications, forms and instructions

Publications provide explanations and examples of the IRS's interpretation of a particular tax provision. They are meant to assist taxpayers in preparing tax returns and forms and are therefore written in plain English. Whether it's how to deduct charitable contributions or which expenses count as itemized deductions, the average individual taxpayer will at some point in his or her life look at an IRS publication. But these publications are not meant to be the law and should not be considered as binding legal authority or precedent.

Instructions typically accompany a tax form and provide line-by-line detail on filling out the form. Sometimes instructions can be quite lengthy. According to the National Taxpayers Union, the 2003 instructions for Form 1040A were some 85 pages long – and that is supposed to be the IRS's short form. The regular Form 1040 comes with 126 pages of instructions. All in all, the IRS prints some 1,101 publications, forms and instructions, amounting to approximately 16,339 pages.

Internal Revenue Manual

The Internal Revenue Manual (IRM) is the IRS's internal policy book. It is written by IRS employees for other IRS agents to use when administering tax laws and procedures.

Internal Revenue Bulletin

The Internal Revenue Bulletin (IRB) is the IRS's weekly publication listing various IRS pronouncements – announcements, rules and procedures. When it is consolidated into an annual form it's called the Cumulative Bulletin.

Treasury decisions

Treasury decisions are used to adopt final Treasury regulations. They provide helpful background information on those regulations.

The Courts

Sometimes the IRS and a taxpayer will not agree on a particular tax issue. This typically occurs when the IRS is auditing the taxpayer. Such tax disputes are fought mainly in three courts:

- *U.S. Tax Court*
- *U.S. Court of Federal Claims*
- *U. S. District Court*

The IRS may be represented in court by attorneys from the U.S. Department of Justice, Tax Division, commonly referred to as the Tax Division. The Tax Division is located in Washington, D.C. Attorneys with the IRS Chief Counsel's Office in Washington, D.C., and at local regional offices may also be involved in cases either as actual representatives or as consultants. Taxpayers may be represented by attorneys but often represent themselves, appearing pro se.

U.S. Tax Court

The United States Tax Court was established by Congress in 1924; at that time, it was called the U.S. Board of Tax Appeals. Its purpose is to decide controversies between taxpayers and the IRS. There are 19 judges on the tax court, all appointed by the president. The court is located in Washington, D.C., although judges will travel to hear cases in certain cities around the country. There is no jury in Tax Court. Taxpayers may be represented by attorneys or others who are qualified to practice in front of the Tax Court. They may also represent themselves. The government is typically represented by attorneys from the IRS. Although taxpayers must pay a minor filing fee, they can file a case in Tax Court without having to pay the alleged tax deficiency first. This is not the case for the other two venues discussed below.

U.S. Court of Federal Claims

The current United States Court of Federal Claims was created by Congress in 1982. This court is authorized to preside over money claims based upon the United Sates Constitution, federal statutes, executive regulations or contracts with the United States. Approximately one-fourth of all cases involve tax refunds. The Court of Federal Claims is located in Washington, D.C., although judges also travel to hear cases in certain cities around the country. Sixteen judges appointed by the president serve for 15-year terms. Jury trials are not available. The government is typically represented by attorneys from the Department of Justice, Tax Division. The alleged tax deficiency must be paid before a case will be heard by the court.

U.S. District Court

The United States District Court is a federal trial-level court, with separate courts located in all 50 states. Unlike the Tax Court and the Court of Federal Claims, jury trials are available in federal district court. In a tax case, the government is typically represented by attorneys from the Justice Department's Tax Division, and the taxpayer must pay the alleged tax deficiency before her case will be heard.

Key Tax Doctrines

Over the years, several major principles have emerged that serve as the backbone for U.S. tax laws. These principles, known as "tax doctrines," have been critical in shaping the tax law industry as we know it. Most, if not all, of these doctrines have been developed by court cases. A good source for many of these doctrines and the basic legal tax theories is provided in *Chirelstein's Federal Income Taxation: A Law Student's Guide to Leading Cases and Concepts*, by Marvin Chirelstein. Craig Boise, a tax professor at Case Law School in Cleveland, Ohio, says that Chirelstein's book "is an extremely valuable supplement to the basic textbook for anyone taking their first tax class in law school. It illustrates the fundamental principles of tax law and the more important tax cases with clarity and helpful examples." In fact many commentators liken Chirelstein to the student's "tax law bible." Fenwick & West attorney Allen Madison agrees that a working knowledge of these tax doctrines is critical to anyone interested in practicing tax law. He discusses many of these doctrines in his article, "The Tension Between Textualism and Substance-Over-Form Doctrines in Tax Law," published in Volume 43, Number 3 of the Santa Clara Law Review.

What follows is an overview, but by no means an exhaustive list, of some of the basic tax doctrines.

Realization doctrine

When should you have to pay taxes on your income? Most people think the answer to this is simple. If you work in 2002 you should pay taxes on that money on your 2002 tax return. But what if you don't actually get paid in 2002? Instead you receive the check for this work in 2003.

Under the realization doctrine, income is not taxed until it is realized. Section 61 of the Code states in part, "Except as otherwise provided in this subtitle, gross income means all income from whatever source derived, including (but not limited to) the following items...." Relevant regulations define gross income as "income realized in any form, whether in money, property, or services." The realization principle helps you decide when – meaning in which year – your income will be taxed. A taxpayer generally must pay tax on income in the year it is received or accrued. If you receive a paycheck in 2003 for work performed in 2002, you don't treat (i.e., realize) that money as income until your 2003 tax return.

Assignment of income

Under the assignment of income doctrine, the person who actually earns the income is subject to taxation and not the person who may eventually receive the income. In this way a parent cannot avoid paying income taxes on his wages by having his employer pay his check directly to his child, who coincidentally happens to be in a lower tax bracket. Obviously if it were that simple, everyone would have their kids on the payroll from the time they could stand up.

Step transaction

The step transaction doctrine is like mending a broken ladder. The theory is that a series of different steps should be put together to form one cohesive story – hence the mended ladder. For example, assume X owns property and wants to sell it and use the loss to decrease his income from other sources. X devises a plan to sell the property to Y, a related party, and then Y agrees to sell it back immediately to X. Under the step transaction doctrine it can be argued that because X didn't realize any change in ownership he shouldn't be able to recognize a loss. The two transactions would be lumped together as one and hence result in no loss for X. The step transaction does not apply if it can be shown that the steps have an independent business purpose apart from tax avoidance.

Tax benefit doctrine

Millions of people are faced with the tax benefit rule every year when they prepare their tax return and they don't even know it. Here's how it works. If you take a deduction in one year and later in a subsequent year recover that deduction, you received a tax benefit – because your net position is better off from a tax standpoint. This happens often when taxpayers who itemize take deductions, such as state income taxes, and then subsequently receive a tax refund from their state. If you deduct $5,000 worth of state income taxes on your federal income tax return and then wind up getting a $1,500 state tax refund, you received a tax benefit by being able to deduct the entire $5,000 when you were only out of pocket $3,500. Under the tax benefit doctrine, the $1,500 will have to be included in your income on your next federal income tax return. So the next time you get a Form 1099-G from your state listing the amount of your tax refund, know that it is the tax benefit doctrine at work.

Substance over form

There are many times in life when what is formally written or recorded does not really convey the true facts. In the context of tax transactions, there is typically some written agreement, memorandum or other document that serves as the form, but is this the true substance of what the parties agreed to? For example, a loan agreement between a parent and a child may provide that the child will pay the parent back over a certain period of time and at a certain interest rate. But even though there is a formal loan document, the parent and child may never intend for the child to repay the loan. Thus, in substance the parent really gave the child a gift. Accordingly, under this doctrine, the substance of the transaction (a gift) should be used and not its rigid form (a loan).

Sham transaction/economic substance

A sham transaction is defined as a business transaction that is entered into for the purpose of avoiding tax. Under the tax rules, sham transactions are ignored and the desired tax treatment is not achieved because the transactions are said to lack economic substance. In evaluating a transaction that may potentially be a sham, courts typically look at whether the transaction was negotiated at arm's length, whether the price for the deal was inflated and whether the overall financial structure of the deal and the contractual terms are actually being followed by the parties.

In recent years the sham transaction/economic substance doctrine has been cited in the popular press as one important reason for so many corporate failures. The Enron debacle had many commentators fuming about alleged sham transactions that were used to help Enron avoid paying federal income taxes. Enron had some 900 subsidiaries that were located in several so-called tax-haven countries. It used these subsidiaries to create certain partnerships whereby the actual profits from the partnership were given to (or "allocated" in the tax world) the partners, like banks, who were not subject to U.S. income taxes. Then these profits were returned to Enron in the United States ("repatriated") tax-free under other transactions.

Having subsidiaries, even several, in tax-haven countries engaged in these partnerships does not, standing alone, indicate that the transactions were shams that lack economic substance. However, the sheer number of subsidiaries used by Enron, along with the other allegations of corporate and accounting impropriety, has caused Congress, the IRS and the Treasury

Department to scrutinize these arrangements carefully. In 2003, federal legislation was introduced to formalize the economic substance doctrine.

Business purpose doctrine

Along with the substance-over-form, sham transaction and economic substance doctrines, courts have attacked transactions that lack any real purpose but the avoidance of taxes under the business purpose doctrine. Under this doctrine, a transaction that literally follows the tax laws but serves no real commercial or business purposes, other than the reduction or elimination of taxes, will not receive the desired tax treatment. For example, assume a taxpayer takes out a loan from a related party and the terms provide for an interest rate of 12 percent. The taxpayer will get an interest deduction of 12 percent to use in reducing income from other sources. Now assume the taxpayer invests the loan amount in an interest-bearing account that earns 4 percent. This 4 percent interest will represent interest income to the taxpayer. The net between the two, a deduction of 12 percent and income of 4 percent, is an 8 percent deduction. It could be argued that the taxpayer only entered this transaction for tax purposes to generate a tax loss – that the transaction did not serve any legitimate business purpose.

To get the best law jobs, you need the best legal career advice.

That's where Vault's expertise in the legal field can help you. We wrote the book on top law firms. Now we can help you reach the next stage in your legal career.

Law Resume Writing and Resume Reviews

- Have your resume reviewed by a legal resume expert.
- For resume writing, start with an e-mailed history and 1- to 2-hour phone discussion. Our experts will write a first draft, and deliver a final draft after feedback and discussion.
- For resume reviews, get an in-depth, detailed critique and rewrite within TWO BUSINESS DAYS.

Law Career Coaching

Need Vault's help in solving a pressing legal career question? We've got experts ready to assist you.

- Looking to leave Big Law?
- Ready to move to another law firm?
- Considering a switch from private practice to government work?
- Just graduating from law school and unsure where to begin?

"It was well worth the price! I have been struggling with this for weeks and in 48 hours you had given me the answers! I now know what I need to change."

-- T.H., Attorney, Pasadena, CA

"Law school taught me to be precise, your comments helped me to see the bigger picture and make the resume more accessible to a hiring manager."

-- A.J., Recent Law School Graduate, Chicago, IL

"Thank you for your time and patience, I really felt like you heard what I had to say and made great suggestions!"

-- R.F., Attorney, Chicago, IL

For more information go to
www.vault.com/law

VAULT
> the most trusted name in career information™

Tax Lawyers in All Shapes and Sizes

CHAPTER 2

As if being a tax lawyer weren't specialized enough, this area of law is famous for its subspecialties. In fact, choosing to be a tax lawyer is just the beginning. Tax laws have become so complex that gone are the days of being a tax generalist – someone who knows a little something about many tax areas. Depending on the job and the organization (law firm, accounting firm, government), tax lawyers might be forced to subspecialize.

Who They Are

Tax lawyers typically fall into four main types: (1) those who come up with and develop transactions, also known as planners; (2) those who advocate a position for a client with a taxing authority like the IRS and sometimes litigate this position in court, known as controversy experts; (3) those who actually complete and file tax returns, known as compliance experts; and (4) certain hybrids who do a little bit of everything, including planning, controversy, compliance and legislation. In addition, tax lawyers are often then further divided by their tax specialty.

Planners

Tax lawyers who plan transactions, typically with a goal of eliminating or minimizing taxes, are known as planners. Planners may help structure or organize a transaction before it occurs. For example, a planner might help in the structuring of a merger or an acquisition. Here's how this might work: Corporation A wants to purchase Corporation B. The tax planner, who is engaged by Corporation A, will likely be part of a structuring team that consists of corporate lawyers, accountants, investment bankers and business people. She will be charged with figuring out how to structure the deal in the most tax-efficient manner for Corporation A.

Planners may also be involved with a transaction after it has occurred. For example, three guys with the next great web site decide to form a company. They consult with a tax planner and decide to use a limited liability company because it's only subject to one level of tax. They form the 3 Guys LLC. But now they believe that they are on the verge of being the next eBay and want to go public to get more resources to take them to the next level. Since only

C corporations can engage in public offerings, 3 Guys LLC needs to merge into a new C corporation. A tax planner will likely be consulted during the unwinding of the 3 Guys LLC in order to help avoid certain taxes.

Planners document their ideas and techniques in contracts, agreements and memoranda. They typically do not complete or file the actual tax return that reflects their planning.

Controversy attorneys

Of all the varieties of tax lawyer, controversy attorneys are those most likely to experience the heady rush of courtroom cross-examination. At a time when accounting and corporate improprieties continue to make headlines, tax controversy attorneys are likely to see more action in the courtroom as their clients' accounting and tax plans face investigation and attack. Tax controversy attorneys help their clients defend tax matters – generally conflicts over the amount or type of tax owed. This defense can start as early as when the planners structure the deal.

Controversy tax attorneys may work with planners to make sure that the transaction is structured in line with current tax cases. They also help clients prepare for tax audits. These audits generally start when information document requests (IDRs) are issued by the IRS or a state or local tax authority. IDRs seek detailed tax and business information from the taxpayer. Once the audit is completed, the IRS writes up its notice of proposed assessment (NOPA) which highlights the auditor's findings and how much, if any, taxes are owed. At this point the controversy attorney may help write an appeal of these findings in the form of a legal brief known as a protest. This protest is filed with the IRS Appeals Division, commonly referred to as Appeals, or with a similar body when dealing with a state or local taxing authority.

The taxpayer may decide to forgo the IRS appeals process altogether and have his day in court. Taxpayers have three choices of venue for fighting tax matters – Tax Court, the Court of Federal Claims or federal district court. In this context, controversy attorneys act like litigators. They interview witnesses, review boxes and boxes of documents, research legal theories, draft legal briefs and present the taxpayer's case at trial. Controversy attorneys also defend clients accused of violating criminal tax laws.

Compliance experts

When most people think of taxes they think of April 15th. But many tax lawyers, other than those who actually prepare tax returns, don't know anything more about income tax returns than the average person. This specialized tax return preparation business is known as "compliance." Tax preparation services have become a big business, an industry worth an estimated $225 billion a year, according to an April 16, 2000, speech given by Rep. Zach Wamp, R-Tenn.

Compliance specialists prepare tax returns for individuals, corporations, partnerships, trust and estates, and just about anyone who needs to file a tax return. They file these returns with the federal government, state and local governments, and even foreign countries. They also interact with accountants who prepare financial statements, as there are often differences between how something is reflected on a tax return versus how it must be described under generally accepted accounting principles (GAAP) on a financial statement.

Hybrids

Some tax lawyers do a combination of things – some planning, some controversy and some compliance. A prime example of this is the group of tax lawyers who formulate tax policy and legislation. John O'Neill, director of TaxTalent.com, an online career management and resource center devoted to tax professionals, notes that "tax lawyers who do legislation and policy work often start out with something that a planner did, then due to some sort of controversy they discover a tax loophole, and then they must draft tax legislation to close the loophole while keeping an eye to how compliance preparers will now abide by and report this change in tax laws on the tax returns."

A recent example of such reactive tax legislation can be found in wake of the Enron scandal, in the so-called Bermuda inversion transaction. Enron used these inversion transactions (developed by planners) to reduce its U.S. taxable income. Here's how it works. A U.S. corporation forms a subsidiary in a tax-haven country like Bermuda. Under a series of carefully planned steps, the foreign subsidiary then becomes the parent of the U.S. corporation – the ownership relationship is thus inverted. This allows the U.S. corporation to eliminate taxes on everything but its U.S.-based operations.

After the fall of Enron, the IRS became very interested in these inversion transactions, which spawned a fair amount of controversy work. Congress also began investigating these transactions and was outraged at how they resulted in significant decreases in U.S. taxes. Some legislators even called the transactions "unpatriotic." New legislation curbing the tax benefits realized from these transactions is certainly on the horizon. The tax attorneys working on this legislation will be wearing several hats – as planners to understand the effects of the legislation, as controversy attorneys in foreseeing how these transactions can be detected and audited, and finally as return preparers in determining how these transactions should be reflected on tax returns.

At the state level, these tax lawyers often work on appropriations bills for more funding during the state budgeting process. For example, Randle Pollard, domestic tax counsel with a major pharmaceutical company, says he "worked on legislation to extend certain corporate tax credits at the state level and to eliminate certain property taxes on businesses. The key to passing this legislation was getting the legislature to agree that these incentives help attract and retain high-growth businesses in the state, which in turn helps create more jobs in the state. It was also important to understand the balance of creating an attractive environment for businesses without unduly burdening individual taxpayers or harming the state budget."

This kind of work requires knowing something about tax planning in order to determine how the property tax elimination might impact the companies. It also includes assessing possible controversy issues around how the change in the law might be handled under an audit by the proper state taxing authority. Finally, there is an element of compliance work in figuring out how the companies might prepare tax returns in light of the proposed legislation.

Tax Specialties

As if dividing up tax lawyers by the kind of practice weren't enough, tax lawyers are also divided into the different areas on which they focus. The American Bar Association's Section of Taxation, the largest professional organization of tax lawyers, has over 40 active committees based on substantive tax areas, including the following:

- Banking and Savings Institutions
- Civil and Criminal Tax Penalties
- Closely Held Businesses
- Corporate Tax
- Court Procedure and Practice
- Domestic Relations
- Employee Benefits

- Employment Taxes
- Energy & Environmental Taxes
- Estate and Gift Taxes
- Exempt Organizations
- Fiduciary Income Tax
- Financial Transactions
- Foreign Activities of U.S. Taxpayers
- Individual income tax
- Insurance Companies
- Low Income Taxpayers
- Partnerships and LLCs
- Real Estate
- S Corporations
- State and Local Taxes
- Tax Accounting
- Transfer Pricing
- U.S. Activities of Foreigners and Tax Treaties

So a tax attorney might be a planner who specializes in partnerships, often referred to as a Subchapter K attorney because partnerships are covered in Subchapter K of the Internal Revenue Code. Or a tax lawyer might be a controversy attorney who specializes in international tax matters. There are many combinations – more than the choices for a latte at Starbucks. The following gives an overview of some of the tax areas in which attorneys practice.

Subchapter K

A partnership is an entity formed when two or more people (or other entities) get together and agree to transact business. This agreement can be oral or formalized in a written document. Partnership tax attorneys work on planning partnership structures as well as drafting documents to memorialize the partnership agreements. In recent years they have also worked with limited liability companies since these entities are subject to the same partnership tax rules found in Subchapter K of the Tax Code. As one lawyer in the Northeast explains, "Many partnership tax attorneys also work on real estate transactions – either with large corporations like Real Estate Investment Trusts (REITs) or with high-wealth individuals. Also, partnership tax has become more prevalent with the growing popularity of limited liability companies and corporate joint venturing."

Partnership tax attorneys also work closely with tax attorneys in other subspecialties such as estate planning. Many estate plans involve closely held businesses, which are often partnerships or limited liability companies. These attorneys are also referred to as pass-through experts since they deal with other entities besides partnerships, like S corporations, all of which "pass through" their tax income and liabilities to their owners. These pass-through entities may file federal income tax returns, but they don't pay taxes on these returns. In fact, their federal income tax returns are called informational returns.

Subchapter C or corporate

Corporate tax attorneys typically work on transactions that involve Subchapter C corporations. A C corporation is taxed under Subchapter C of the Internal Revenue Code; it is a legal entity separate and distinct from its stockholders, the owners of the corporation. These transactions may deal with forming the entity, but they can also involve merging two corporations or dissolving a corporation as well.

Corporate tax attorneys often work closely with a corporation's finance and in-house tax departments. They are typically planners or they focus on corporate compliance issues. They also interact with other attorneys, like general corporate and securities attorneys, in structuring deals, and they work with the company's accounting firm to understand any impact that the transaction may have on the company's financial statements. A tax attorney with a top New York law firm explains his responsibilities: "As a corporate attorney I structure, negotiate and draft mergers and acquisitions, restructurings (in and out of bankruptcy), and debt/equity/hybrid offerings. There's a lot of client contact. Although the transactions tend to be fast-tracked, the experiences are rich."

Financial institutions and products

Tax lawyers who practice in the field of financial institutions or products, known as FIP, evaluate the tax consequences of issuing and buying debt instruments, stocks, options, and entering into derivative contracts and hedging. These attorneys look at the tax consequences of investing in the stock market and whether the proposed transaction will be treated as ordinary income or capital gains. Richard Larkins, a partner with Ernst & Young LLP who specializes in FIP, explains that "FIP attorneys mostly work with large corporations like investment banks or Fortune 500 companies who are issuing debt." They also represent wealthy individuals.

As companies get involved in more global investments and transactions, FIP attorneys work on the deals – known as "cross-border" transactions – with corporate and international lawyers. FIP attorneys also often work closely with M&A attorneys in structuring the financing for corporate deals.

Exempt organizations

Tax lawyers who represent exempt organizations are known as EO attorneys. Exempt organizations can include organizations as large as universities, hospitals, labor unions, trade associations and corporate or family private foundations. But they also include churches, smaller advocacy organizations and local charities. Eve Borenstein, an exempt organizations lawyer in Minneapolis, says that "exempt organization work offers an attorney the ability to take the public policy that Congress has set with respect to nonprofit organizations and apply it to helping these organizations."

Many exempt organization attorneys handle tax issues for 501(c)(3) organizations, often called charities. Borenstein says that 80 percent of her practice comes from helping charities. But there are many other kinds of nonprofits such as fraternal organizations, social clubs, social welfare organizations, trade associations, country clubs and even labor unions.

State and local taxes

State and local taxes, known as SALT, has become an important area for tax lawyers. Many states and localities impose taxes on their residents to raise monies to maintain their governments and for a host of local initiatives. These taxes include income taxes, property taxes and sales taxes. As states become more and more aggressive in drafting and enforcing tax laws, tax attorneys have developed a cottage industry in planning and defending their clients under these laws.

SALT attorneys work on myriad issues such as whether or not a state has "nexus" (i.e., enough minimum contacts) to tax a particular client. Randle Pollard, who works in-house at a large pharmaceutical company, discusses the nature of his practice: "As a state and local tax attorney, I defend the filing position of the company for particular states and provide tax planning and saving ideas for future state tax return filings. To do this job, you don't need to know the state tax laws in all 50 states, but you do need to understand some overall concepts such as whether a state has nexus and does the state use a unitary or a worldwide taxing scheme." SALT attorneys also represent high net-worth individuals like athletes, entertainers and expatriates (American citizens working abroad) to help them minimize their state tax burden and handle compliance work. Finally, SALT attorneys also help their clients comply with property taxes, sales and use taxes, local taxes and licensing fees.

Income tax and accounting

Income tax and accounting (IT&A) attorneys deal with recognition and timing of income and deductions by individuals and corporations. They also handle transactions involving the tax treatment of sales or exchanges, capital gains and losses, accounting methods and periods, installment sales, long-term contracts, inventories and alternative minimum tax. In recent years the alternative minimum tax area has created a lot of work for these attorneys. The alternative minimum tax (AMT) is a separate tax system that parallels the regular income taxing system, with numerous modifications, exemptions and adjustments. Every taxpayer must compute both his regular income tax and his AMT. Whichever results in the greater amount is his tax liability.

The AMT first took affect in 1970 to ensure that the truly wealthy paid their share of the federal tax burden. At that time, testimony to Congress by then – Treasury Secretary Joseph W. Barr noted that 155 high-income households had paid no income tax at all in 1966 because of their use of tax loopholes. The AMT was meant to apply to a small percentage of the American population that had avoided paying their share of taxes. However, because the AMT exemption amounts have not been indexed for inflation since 1970, the Joint Committee on Taxation estimates that some 30 million "average" taxpayers will be subject to the AMT. IT&A attorneys help their clients plan for ways to decrease, and if possible eliminate, the AMT.

Estate and gift tax

The estate tax taxes property held by a person at the time of her death. Currently, the first $1 million in value of a deceased person's estate can be passed tax-free to her heirs. Estates valued at more than $1 million are subject to estate taxes. Gift taxes apply a tax to the value of gifts given by one individual to another. There are many exceptions to this tax such as gifts between spouses and payments of college tuition if the payments are made directly to the institution. Currently, the first $11,000 of a gift can be given by any one individual to another individual on a tax-free basis.

As the population ages, estate and gift tax becomes a very popular area. According to a report issued by the U.S. Department of Labor, there are over 70 million Americans who qualify as baby boomers – those born between the years of 1946 and 1964. This translates into roughly one-third of the U.S. population, a large market of people in need of estate planning services.

According to Melinda Merk, a tax manager at a Big Four accounting firm in Washington, D.C., "Estate planning can help clients transfer their wealth in accordance with their goals and objectives, while saving estate and gift taxes, as well as income taxes. It can also help clients plan for their financial future." Many estate planning attorneys also draft wills and trusts. As Merk notes, "There is a significant non-tax piece that goes with the tax side of estate planning. The estate planning process typically involves a team of advisors, including the client's estate planning attorney, investment advisor, insurance agent and tax advisor."

There have been numerous legislative proposals to do away with the estate tax. In June 2003, the House of Representatives passed a bill to repeal the estate tax. Although no one knows for certain what will happen to these legislative proposals, John O'Neill believes that "because of uncertainty of the laws, this could be a risky area for a tax practitioner." On the other hand, Merk seems less concerned. "I'm not worried about federal estate tax repeal," she says. "Even if this were to happen, people would still have to plan for where they want their assets to go at their death. Also, most states will still continue to impose an estate tax at the state level."

International tax

International tax law is perhaps the hottest area in tax right now. TaxTalent.com's John O'Neill believes that "over the long term, an international tax specialist can make an annual 15 percent premium over a general tax person." These lawyers work on tax planning issues for global companies and high net-worth individuals. They work closely with other tax lawyers like corporate and partnership attorneys and often have direct client contact with business people. Some international tax lawyers are experts in the tax laws of other countries.

Professor Craig Boise at Case Law School in Cleveland focuses on international tax issues. He describes international tax practice as "helping clients understand the U.S. federal income tax treatment of transactions that cross international borders." He observes that there are two components to international taxation: taxation of "outbound transactions" – business activities of U.S. persons undertaken abroad – and taxation of "inbound transactions" – business activities of foreign persons undertaken within the United States. In each of these areas, he notes, tax practitioners may add value by assisting clients in minimizing their tax liability through careful structuring of business activities to the extent allowed by the Internal Revenue Code and Treasury regulations.

Employee benefits

Employee benefits is another growing area for tax attorneys and a very big subspecialty. While some employment attorneys also concentrate on employee benefits, tax attorneys approach the subject from a different perspective. Lisa Tavares, a tax associate with a Washington, D.C., law firm, explains the difference: "These tax attorneys work with the tax-related provisions of ERISA, while labor attorneys deal with the rights and claims for benefits under ERISA. The tax provisions include such things as what employers or plan sponsors have to do to get a tax deduction through providing benefit plans. For example, an employer cannot discriminate and provide better benefits in favor of highly compensated employees. Basically, you can't give more benefits and perks to the CEO than to the secretary. If the employer doesn't follow these rules, the employee will have to pay taxes on the amounts they contributed to the benefit plan – not the result that most companies who want to retain their workforce want to happen. Thus, a lot of my time is spent making sure that clients comply with ERISA."

Employment taxes

Anyone who has ever had a job is familiar with employment taxes: Medicare, Social Security, federal unemployment taxes and state unemployment taxes. The Federal Insurance Contribution Act (FICA) is a federal law requiring employers to withhold two separate taxes from employees' wages, Social Security and Medicare. Medicare taxes provide medical benefits for certain individuals when they reach age 65. Federal unemployment taxes and state unemployment taxes are used to help with the administration of federal and state unemployment insurance programs. Social Security taxes provide benefits for retired workers, the disabled and the dependents of both.

Tax attorneys in this area deal with a variety of issues including where employment or payroll taxes must be paid (i.e., to which states and/or the federal government) and by whom. They also help determine whether or not someone who is working with an employer is actually an employee or an independent contractor. The distinction becomes important to employers because with an independent contractor the employer does not have to withhold employment taxes. Nor does the employer have to match the amount of applicable employment taxes. With employees, on the other hand, the employer not only has to withhold employment taxes from their paychecks, but the employer must also pay a matching amount of employment taxes.

As companies face a downturn in the economy and see their debts mounting, they sometimes borrow against the employment tax fund, with the thought that they will have the money to remit to the IRS when the taxes are due (typically quarterly). But the IRS is serious about collecting employment taxes – so much so that it might go after the personal assets of the president or others in charge of withholding and paying employment taxes. Thus, employment tax lawyers may find themselves doing controversy work in defending their clients against employment tax audits and in negotiating arrangements for clients who are delinquent paying these taxes.

Where They Work

Tax attorneys have various career options available to them. The next chapter will provide greater details as to what tax attorneys in different positions actually do, but the following offers a brief overview of the organizations where many tax attorneys work.

Government

Many tax lawyers get their start in the profession by working for the government. While the Internal Revenue Service is the primary government employer, tax attorneys also might work for the Treasury Department, the United States Tax Court or a congressional representative, senator or congressional committee.

Law firms

There are thousands of law firms in the United States alone. Many medium-sized and large law firms have at least one or two tax attorneys on staff. At very large law firms there is often a fully staffed tax department, handling a variety tax specialties. For example, the mammoth firm of Baker & McKenzie has more than 450 tax attorneys in over 35 offices worldwide.

In general, tax departments in law firms tend to be less specialized than those in accounting firms. Law firm tax attorneys may research issues ranging from partnership concepts one day to international tax issues the next. As a tax attorney becomes more senior in the law firm, she usually begins to specialize in a particular area of tax law.

Accounting firms

Since the late 1980s and in the wake of the Enron scandal, large accounting firms have gone through a period of consolidation. Where eight accounting firms led the pack in the 1980s, in 2003, four global accounting firms remain, known in the United States as PricewaterhouseCoopers LLP, Deloitte & Touche LLP, Ernst & Young LLP, and KPMG LLP. There are also many regional accounting firms that hire tax lawyers.

Unlike law firms, accounting firms tend to divide their work along particular tax specialties. The young tax lawyer at an accounting firm will need to choose a particular tax area in which to specialize.

Corporations

Some tax attorneys choose to go in-house and work for a corporation. Most Fortune 500 corporations have in-house tax departments staffed with a mixture of tax lawyers and tax accountants. Many of these lawyers are planners and/or controversy attorneys. Some tax lawyers also do compliance work. Corporations tend to hire experienced tax lawyers – typically those with a minimum of three to five years of experience, preferably with a law firm or an accounting firm.

Other tax attorneys go in-house with nonprofit corporations. Note that nonprofit does not necessarily mean small. Nonprofit organizations include major colleges and universities, hospitals and health care organizations, as well as private foundations. These in-house tax specialists typically work in the exempt organizations and/or estate planning area.

Academia

Some tax lawyers go back to law school, only this time as professors. Those who teach tax law typically have a keen interest in writing tax-related articles and books. Because they also make presentations at seminars and conferences; tax professors are generally experienced public speakers with excellent writing skills.

Psst...
Need a Change in Venue?

Use the Internet's most targeted job search tools for law professionals.

Vault Law Job Board
The most comprehensive and convenient job board for law professionals. Target your search by area of law, function, and experience level, and find the job openings that you want. No surfing required.

VaultMatch Resume Database
Vault takes match-making to the next level: post your resume and customize your search by area of law, experience and more. We'll match job listings with your interests and criteria and e-mail them directly to your inbox.

VAULT
> the most trusted name in career information™

Taxing Trends

CHAPTER 3

For most of the 2003 graduating classes, the news is bleak on the job market front. According to the National Association of Colleges and Employers, 42.4 percent of surveyed employers plan to hire fewer graduates than they did last year. This means a decline of approximately 3.6 percent in job opportunities for the class of 2003. But does the same dismal outlook hold true for tax positions? Will rumors of tax reforms, financial fraud and corporate bankruptcies make the field obsolete?

Jobs, Jobs and More Jobs

In reference to the new American Constitution in 1789, Benjamin Franklin wrote, "Everything appears to promise that it will last; but in this world, nothing can be said to be certain, except death and taxes." His words have never been truer. And with the certainty of taxes comes the even greater need for tax professionals. Experts now predict that there will be a shortage of tax professionals until 2026. To fully appreciate why there will be such a shortage, it is helpful to review the trends in the overall workforce.

According to a 1999 article by Tony Santiago and Eve Abrams, tax-recruiting experts with TaxSearch, Inc., there will be overall workforce shortages due to the decrease in birth rates. In other words, there are more jobs than qualified workers. In fact, the demographics indicate that by 2005, there will be some 15 percent more jobs than people to fill them. Moreover, even if birth rates did increase, there would still be a labor shortage through 2015.

The impact of this labor shortage has an even more dramatic impact on specialized professions like tax. As Santiago observes, "In addition to the overall labor shortage, we see in the tax field that less people are going into the accounting field, which yields less people who are likely to pick tax out of that pool. Also, there is a dearth of technically competent people who can communicate in a non-technical manner, the truly creative and out-of-the-box thinkers. Finally, tax is not a portable profession – we have to rely almost exclusively on U.S. trained folks. Knowledge by foreign tax professionals doesn't fit in. It's not like with engineers who can come from another country and the general principles still apply."

But the current unemployment rates in 2003 seem to suggest that, at least in the short term, there are more people than jobs available. Wayne Hamilton, a tax attorney in Florida, believes that "the job market for tax attorneys doing planning for transactional, corporate-type work is slow because there simply aren't as many top-tier corporate transactions – not like in the peak of the dot-com days." He adds that "for tax lawyers doing controversy work, the job market looks somewhat better. The IRS is hiring a lot of new people and they are also auditing more businesses and individuals, so this will create more tax positions as people gear up to defend these audits."

Other practitioners have also witnessed a tighter job market. In the view of a Midwestern tax lawyer, "Things have really slowed down in the job front. But I did get calls from two headhunters over the last few weeks – this is down from at least two calls per week last year. However, I do believe there are still tax jobs out there. You just have to look a bit harder and search a while longer. Besides, it's still a much better job market for a tax lawyer than a general corporate attorney." But one attorney on the East Coast warns that "many big organizations like accounting firms are laying off senior professionals. Even though tax may be safer than general corporate, I have never felt job security – not like with litigation lawyers."

Nevertheless, TaxTalent.com's John O'Neill offers some reassurance. "The good tax professionals will always be working," he says, "even in a down market. Keep in mind that approximately 70 percent of all jobs aren't even advertised. The top people get these jobs through networking. Also, in a down market, people need to be more flexible. There are still tax jobs out there but maybe the location isn't ideal. Instead of waiting around for the international tax position in San Francisco, the opportunity may be in the Midwest."

So what areas do top tax recruiters see as particularly ripe for growth? Tony Santiago suggests the following:

Estate and trusts: Tax experts are sorely needed in this field because of the sheer number of baby boomers with high net worth.

International: This tax area continues to be very busy. Most companies are becoming more global in the way they approach their business. And foreign jurisdictions, like Germany, are getting very sophisticated in drafting and applying their tax laws. All of this leads to more work for the international tax expert.

State and local taxes: The state of California, the fifth-largest economy in the world, had a deficit of over $38 billion dollars at the end of August 2002. Because many states are facing huge deficits, there is a strong market for state and local tax experts who can help draft legislation and collect money.

Flat Tax, National Sales Tax, Value-Added Tax, No Tax

There has been a lot of talk about scrapping the U.S. federal tax system altogether. Suggestions have been made to replace our current tax structure with other taxing authorities. One proposal for a flat tax system would use one tax rate with no deductions so that the effective tax rate remains the same regardless of income. Such a system would only tax income as it was first earned but not investment income. So if you are lucky enough to hit the lottery you would pay tax on your winnings at the flat tax rate but then any interest earned off those winnings would be tax-free. Another proposal, for a national sales tax, would tax sales of services and property, similar to the sales taxes imposed by many states and localities.

Many European countries have a value-added tax system (VAT). With the VAT, the tax is imposed on the product at each stage of production. Thus the business buying the component parts to make the final product actually pays the VAT. By the time the product is ready for sale to the consumer, the final price includes all of the markups for the VATs that were previously paid. The consumer pays the VAT when she buys the product.

These latter two taxes (national sales tax and VAT) are consumption-type taxes in that they look to tax money only when it is spent. Under our current tax system, which is an income taxation system, we focus on taxing money as it is earned, regardless of whether or not it is spent. The flat tax and the consumption tax have been attacked as unfair since they tend to tax the poor more than the rich. Proponents of these taxing systems have suggested that this imbalance could be rectified by including a list of exemptions for the poor for food and necessities so that they needn't pay taxes on these products and services.

Some tax reformers suggest making the federal income tax more progressive, while others would have us do away with taxes altogether. A quick search on the Internet will yield numerous individuals and groups who argue against paying any federal taxes. Several tax reform proposals have been introduced as legislation in Congress although none have passed and few if any senators or representatives have seriously supported the notion that federal taxes should be abolished as unconstitutional. Is this reform legislation likely to go anywhere and, if so, what would these alternative tax structures mean for tax lawyers?

Tony Santiago, president of the boutique recruiting firm, TaxSearch, offers his opinion: "I don't think we will go to a flat tax. You must keep in mind that the Tax Code is often used as a sort of political football. In the end, though, I don't think we would be better off and the system would still be complicated. Also, I don't think that the IRS or the state governments really want a flat tax scheme – in fact, I think they like having all of these differences." An East Coast tax attorney agrees and adds, "Going to some type of alternate system like a flat tax would only make things more complex. By the time we figured out how to administer it, we would have created all types of exceptions and phases-ins such that we are right back to where we started in the first place."

Is it Really All Good?

The seductive appeal of tax law

Is being a tax lawyer leading you to a life of boring, pocket-protector security? Or does it offer a life of glamour and excitement? If life were really like a John Grisham novel, then young, fresh-faced attorneys might face the mob-driven dangers confronted by Harvard grad Mitch McDeere (Tom Cruise) when he joins a suspiciously successful little tax firm in the 1993 film version of *The Firm*. Less glamorous but charismatic in his own way is another on-screen tax attorney, *L.A. Law's* Stuart Markowitz (played by Michael Tucker), the short, chubby lawyer who brought the "Venus butterfly" to life on prime-time television.

Fictional glamour aside, being a tax lawyer has many advantages, not the least of which is the opportunity to make lots of money. Tax law can be a lucrative field. As John O'Neill observes, "There are not many professions where an individual can make in the upper 5 percent of annual income in this country, but tax is one of those areas." He adds, "When you look at what some of the more senior tax executives earn (partners, directors of tax, vice presidents), for the years of work experience and education required, the cost/benefit ratio is quite high. Many make in excess of $300,000 a year in cash and equity through stock options or ownership of their firms and most do not have a six-figure debt load from school to worry about!"

Other advantages to tax practice include its social value. Melinda Merk finds that "the intellectual challenge of being a tax lawyer is a huge advantage over other types of law. You always have something to talk about at cocktail parties, since tax law affects everyone. Also, you are helping people accomplish their goals and objectives, while also saving taxes. So you can concretely show the value you are delivering."

For Indiana lawyer Randle Pollard, there's something to be said for being perceived as an expert. "With tax, there is this great perception that you are an expert because you are in a field that is perceived to be complex and difficult. It also gives you a competitive edge as to getting into firms or corporations." Pete Lowy, a tax attorney with a large corporation, agrees that many options are open to tax lawyers since "one major advantage in the tax field is the diversity of positions for which tax lawyers are qualified. As a tax lawyer, you can work in a traditional law firm, in a corporation, with lobbying firms, with the IRS, with the Treasury Department, with Congress – including the Committee on Joint Taxation, the House Ways and Means Committee, the Senate Finance Committee and for individual senators and representatives. And I'm sure there are more. Tax lawyers have lots of options."

In addition to various positions within the tax field, the training and skills tax lawyers learn are often transferable to other areas of law and business. John O'Neill believes that "practicing as a tax attorney gives you the ability to change fields." Wayne Hamilton, a Florida attorney, couldn't agree more. He recently switched from the tax department of his corporate employer to the legal department as an associate counsel doing corporate work. He says that as a tax attorney he got to interact with employees at all levels of his organization and when an opportunity arose to do something different he was a strong candidate because he knew the company, he knew the people and his solid tax foundation was seen as a plus.

However, one tax attorney warns those who look to tax as a stepping stone, "If you are using tax as a means to an end, you must make sure that you don't stay in tax too long. Once people see you are smart and good at your tax specialty, they will be less likely to take a chance on offering you non-tax opportunities." John O'Neill also sees this as a problem for professionals whom he counsels. "This perception that you are such an expert can hurt you when trying to move to another field, too," he says. "People may perceive you as having no vision and not seeing the big picture. In fact, very few tax attorneys are in management at the leading law firms, corporations or accounting firms. The stronger your communication skills and business acumen, the better your chances to make this change."

Fighting the stereotypes

One of the disadvantages commonly cited by tax professionals is ironically also considered an advantage – the perception that you are extremely smart. Smart people, especially those who are good with figures, can get labeled as dull, numbers-crunching nerds. In the 2003 film, *Bringing Down the House*,

Steve Martin plays an unhappy, uptight tax lawyer until an ex-con played by Queen Latifah enters his life and turned him into a hip, "Mack daddy" estate planner who saves the day.

John O'Neill addresses the uptight, nerdy image: "Put simply, people may think that you are boring, can't think out of the box or show leadership skills." A tax attorney practicing in Washington, D.C., agrees. "I've heard from other lawyers that they think tax lawyers are academically gifted but socially limited. In fact, a recent review by my boss indicated that my colleagues thought of me as a normal lawyer. This was meant to be a compliment."

Similarly, the intellectual demands of the profession, often described as an asset, can also be seen as a hurdle. Melinda Merk, who works for a Big Four accounting firm, explains, "Tax law can be very complex. So much so that I soon began to understand the true meaning of the word 'taxing.' You really need to be precise when giving tax advice because if you are wrong, you could end up costing your client money." Another attorney voices a similar opinion. "In other legal areas you can almost hide out for five or so years doing things like document production and no one will really know how good or bad your work is. But in tax, you need to analyze issues on day one. Thus, there is a lot of scrutiny right away, so you better be prepared."

Recruiter Tony Santiago sees this complexity as a challenge for many considering tax law as a profession. "The tax field is becoming less attractive to those coming out of school because it is constantly changing. After you go to school for years and learn these complex rules, legislation is introduced and the field changes completely. In some cases this legislation completely ends the field, like what happened with those who subspecialized in foreign sales corporations. They now have to learn a completely new regime regarding the tax treatment of property exported from the United States."

Another common complaint voiced by tax attorneys is the forced specialization in a particular area of tax law. John O'Neill observes that "you can be pigeonholed in a specific area of tax without the ability to explore other areas of tax – particularly in highly specialized fields like employee benefits and state and local tax. Thus, if you want to branch out and do something like international tax work, it may be very difficult."

Finally, a tax attorney on the East Coast finds that "one of the major disadvantages of being a tax lawyer is that the tax profession is not as diverse in terms of race, color, gender and so on, as other legal specialties. So you are always the only one – sort of like a trailblazer." A lawyer down South also sees a lack of diversity and suggests that the perception of nerdiness may have some basis in fact. "Certain areas in the tax field can be a bit snobby – international tax is an example that comes to mind. In general, these lawyers don't have many touchy-feely soft skills and are more interested in displaying their superior intellect. For the people skills you have to look to tax areas where the attorneys have more interaction with clients who are individuals, such as in estate planning."

VAULT LAW CAREER LIBRARY

You are reading just one title from Vault's Law Career Library – the complete resource for legal careers. To see a full list of legal career titles, go to law.vault.com.

"With reviews and profiles of firms that one associate calls 'spot on,' [Vault's] guide has become a key reference for those who want to know what it takes to get hired by a law firm and what to expect once they get there."

– *New York Law Journal*

"To get the unvarnished scoop, check out Vault."

– *SmartMoney magazine*

VAULT
> the most trusted name in career information™

"Vault is indispensable for locating insider information."
– *Metropolitan Corporate Counsel*

ON THE JOB

Chapter 4: Job Responsibilities

Chapter 5: Tax Law Employers

Chapter 6: Employer FAQs

Chapter 7: A Day in the Life

Job Responsibilities

CHAPTER 4

So what do tax lawyers actually do everyday? Regardless of the organization, but particularly in law firms, almost all tax lawyers perform tax research.

Research

It all begins with the Code. Pete Lowy, a tax attorney with a large corporation explains, "If I'm familiar with the general area of tax law, I go straight to the Code, then the Treasury regulations, then case law." For areas of tax law that are unfamiliar or to supplement the Code, many attorneys turn to secondary sources that provide overviews, annotations and explanations of the law. A commonly used secondary source is the BNA Tax Management Portfolios. These portfolios, often called BNAs for short, provide detailed overviews of many different tax subjects. They explain the law, cases and rulings pertaining to a particular tax issue and highlight any gray areas within the subject. They also cite to other articles and treatises discussing the same subject. However useful BNAs are, one practitioner advises, "When researching, you should always go to the primary sources first (e.g., the Code, Treasury regulations and case law). Do not simply rely on some author's rendition of the law."

Other attorneys use online research tools offered by CCH Incorporated (CCH) or Research Institute of America (RIA), databases like LexisNexis or Westlaw, or treatises discussing a particular area of law. Randle Pollard, an in-house tax counsel, uses RIA's Checkpoint Database. "It is very user friendly," he says, "and allows you to view BNAs online." Lisa Tavares, an associate with a Washington, D.C., law firm, uses other online search tools. "I take advantage of the training classes from Westlaw and Lexis," she says. "Also, to keep costs down for my clients, I call the toll-free reference attorneys at Lexis or Westlaw before I go online to help formulate my search and to know what libraries I should search in." Allen Madison at Fenwick & West says, "For non-procedural questions, I go to the CCH Standard Federal Tax Reporter first. For procedural issues, I use the Kafka treatise [Kafka and Cavanaugh, Litigation of Federal Civil Tax Controversies] for litigation or the Saltzman treatise [IRS Practice and Procedure] for IRS procedure."

Many tax lawyers learn these researching skills in law school, often in legal research and writing courses as a first-year law student. Some learn on the job as summer clerks. Melinda Merk, who now works at a Big Four accounting firm, explains, "I learned how to research when I clerked for a law firm during my second and third years of law school. It was an insurance defense/litigation firm, so I had to a do a lot of legal writing (e.g., memos, pleadings, appellate briefs)."

Whether a lawyer learns in school or on the job, it is imperative that a tax attorney acquire these research skills early in his or her career and continue to develop them. As Pete Lowy observes, "With electronic research constantly changing and evolving, learning how to research is not a one time-thing. The trend in most companies and firms is to pare down the space and cost of hard copies and move toward more efficient virtual libraries. You have to continually update your skills and keep pace with technology in order to keep your research tools sharp."

Writing

Okay, so you've done your research. Now you need to convey the fruits of your labor to supervisors, colleagues or clients.

In-house memoranda

Research results are often incorporated into formal, internal memoranda. A memorandum typically has the following components (commonly referred to as the IRAC method):

- **Issue.** This is where you frame the purpose of the memorandum, presenting the facts of your client's situation and the question being addressed.

- **Rule.** This section outlines the tax policies, cases, code sections or regulations that must be analyzed in order to answer the question posed.

- **Analysis and discussion.** This is the meat of the memorandum. Here, you will analyze in detail how the issue should be treated under the law. Expect to use a lot of citations to cases, rulings, regulations and code sections. The discussion should walk the reader through the steps by which the writer arrived at the last section – the conclusion.

- **Conclusion.** Here, you reach an answer to the question posed early on. You might also suggest the next steps the client should take.

Controversy documents

For lawyers who do controversy work, research may end up in written briefs filed with a court. Court documents are subject to stringent and specific guidelines as to format, style and content. Lawyers adhere to general rules of citation as well as court-specific rules addressing form. Law students, particularly those that edit law reviews or journals, will become intimately familiar with *A Uniform System of Citation,* more commonly known as "The Bluebook," in reference to the color of its cover.

Tax lawyers also draft written protests for submission to the IRS or state taxing authorities. Pete Lowy explains how to craft a tax protest: "A protest can be viewed as a typical legal brief, without court rules to cramp your style. Like a typical brief, it should set forth the law and facts that demonstrate you are correct (or at least that there are litigation hazards to the government), and, in most instances, it should also address any facts or law that might be viewed as harmful to your case. But unlike a legal brief filed in court, there is no mandated order of presentation or particulars on number of pages or things like that. So you're free to present the case however you think would be most persuasive. Every case is unique and should be treated that way; there is no template or one-size-fits-all way to present a case."

Informal communication

Research results may also be conveyed by informal means such as e-mails, letters, PowerPoint slides, Excel spreadsheets or oral conversations. Such informal communication is often preferred in organizations like corporations, where the tax lawyer deals with business people and other non-lawyers. Randle Pollard, who works in-house with a pharmaceutical company, says, "Most of my work product is in the form of substantive e-mails to my clients. My clients, non-lawyers, are business people that need concise legal advice. They are not interested in long memos that use formal Bluebook citation rules." It is often important that this communication be short and concise. Lawyers can obtain training on how to write like a business person or prepare PowerPoint slides, either through in-house training, by taking classes at a local community college or through an online course.

Contracts

Some tax attorneys also draft contracts. For example, say Company X wants to purchase Company Y. There are several ways to do this from a tax standpoint that can make the acquisition either taxable to the seller or nontaxable. The tax lawyer will first research whether the transaction is taxable. Then an agreement will be drafted reflecting the terms of the deal, including the taxability issue. The tax lawyer may be involved in negotiating all of this and may even write the language that goes into the document. This is a different skill set from that required to write a memorandum. Contract drafting requires less analysis and concentrates on using precise, appropriate legal terminology to convey the terms of the parties' agreement.

Billing

Accounting for all of this time spent researching, writing and drafting is called billing. Although billing is not as important in corporations, the IRS and academia, client-focused businesses like law firms and accounting firms depend on billing since it is how they get paid. Most organizations have some sort of system, either electronic or paper form, whereby the attorney can record the time he or she spends working on a particular client matter. Lisa Tavares, a law firm associate, says, "I bill my time in 10-minute increments using a computer program called Carpe Diem. This software allows me to click on a client name, which starts a timer on my computer. This timer stays on until I click it off. Thus, I know exactly how much time I spent on a particular client matter."

Other attorneys use shorter time frames. Melinda Merk, a tax manager at an accounting firm, explains, "I bill based on every six minutes (e.g., 0.2 hours, 0.3 hours, 0.4 hours). I used to record my time weekly by going back and looking at old e-mails, calendars and so on. Now I'm better at doing it on a daily basis. I enter it right onto my computer/TRAX program. This is definitely the best way to accurately keep track of your time – doing it as you go." Whether they track time at 6- or 10-minute intervals, most attorneys try to enter their time daily and detail what they actually did for the client. Most organizations provide the new attorney with training on how to bill and record time.

Tax Law Employers

CHAPTER 5

Although all tax lawyers may share certain skill sets and use the same research tools, the nature and level of work they perform, as well as the perks and benefits they enjoy, differ depending on where they work. From law firms and accounting firms to corporations and governmental agencies, tax lawyers have myriad options. But each option comes with certain advantages and disadvantages. What some positions provide in salary they may lack in flexibility for personal time and family life. It is therefore important to examine the various paths available before deciding on a particular direction. The typical positions for tax attorneys are found in one of the following kinds of organization:

- Law firms
- Accounting firms
- Government
- Corporations
- Academia

Because tax law is so specialized, Tony Santiago of TaxSearch, Inc. suggests to those entering the profession, "When you enter the tax field, look at the practice area of your organization to see if it's the type of work you want to do. For example, certain law firms have certain clientele that require specific types of tax work. If, say, the clients really need strong transactional corporate tax expertise and you want to do employee benefits, you either conform to the work at this firm or go to another firm."

Law Firms

"Great training," "excellent research and writing skills," and "valuable negotiation skills" are just some of the advantages of starting a career at a law firm. Tax attorneys at law firms work on a range of matters such as writing memoranda and briefs, researching complex tax issues, and drafting contracts and other documents. More junior associates develop research and writing skills while senior associates typically have more client contact and spend more time trying to develop business.

Law firms come in all shapes and sizes. In this section we will review three main kinds of law practices:

- Big law firms (for purposes of this book, big law firms mean those with at least 400 attorneys and several offices in major cities)

- Medium-sized law firms, many of which serve regional markets
- Solo practitioners

The big boys

The tax departments in large law firms often have 20 or more attorneys. For example, Kirkpatrick & Lockhart, LLP, a Pittsburgh-based firm with over 700 attorneys across the country, has some 25 or more attorneys practicing in tax and trusts and estates. Other large law firms have massive tax departments known for their specialty in a particular area of tax. For example, Baker & McKenzie, LLP has 3,200 attorneys worldwide – with more than 450 lawyers in the tax department. Although these tax attorneys specialize in every area, Baker & McKenzie is particularly known for its expertise in international taxation.

Money, money, money

Law firm salaries vary from city to city. FindLaw's web site (http://careers.findlaw.com/) provides salary comparisons by city and state for many major law firms. In many big cities, base salaries for first-year associates start at $110,000 and go as high as $140,000 a year. In return, these attorneys are expected to bill somewhere between 2,000 and 2,200 hours a year. But bear in mind that billable hours are not the same as work hours; billable hours mean only the hours spent working on matters that can actually be charged to a client. What about all those hours spent on other related and necessary, yet nonetheless non-billable matters? A tax attorney on the East Coast says, "I probably work 400 to 500 hours a year more than what I bill to clients because a fair amount of time is spent on administrative matters like going to firm lunches, continuing education classes and seminars, pro bono activities and client development. None of this, of course, is billable, but all of it is necessary to my practice."

More experienced attorneys at big law firms do quite well, too. Mid-level associates, those who have been practicing from four to six years, typically earn over $150,000. For senior associates, those with seven or more years of experience, earnings can climb over the $200,000 mark! By the time a lawyer reaches the partner level, which can take anywhere from eight years in some firms to 12 or 13 in others, the compensation level, known as profits per partner, begins to vary widely, even within a particular city or metropolitan area. According to the 2003 Survey of Law Firm Economics by Altman Weil, Inc., profits per partner at U.S. law firms averaged $822,814.

Bonuses, benefits and other perks

Most big law firms pay the same base salary to all associates at the same level, regardless of the type of law they practice. But in some firms, specialty areas that are in high demand may command larger starting salaries. For example, according to information on FindLaw, first-year intellectual property lawyers at Dorsey & Whitney LLP make approximately $10,000 more in base salary than other first-year associates at the firm.

Even if base salaries are relatively uniform within a given firm, bonuses and other discretionary perks may differ depending on the practice area. Corporate lawyers who handle a lot of transactions or litigators who work on big cases tend to bill more hours than many tax attorneys. Since bonus structures are often based on billable hours, these attorneys tend to have larger overall compensation packages than tax lawyers.

On the other hand, many tax attorneys don't believe the extra compensation is worth the extra time. This is because, on average, for every additional billable hour that these highly paid associates work to earn a higher bonus, their average hourly rate decreases. Consider the following example:

A tax lawyer and a corporate lawyer both work for a big law firm and have base salaries of $125,000. Assume that this firm requires 2,000 billable hours per year. Associates who reach the 2,000 mark are guaranteed a bonus of $5,000. For every 100 hours billed over 2,000, an associate can receive an additional $5,000, with the total bonus capped at $40,000 for billing up to 2,700. Those who bill more than 2,700 are eligible to receive an additional discretionary bonus.

The tax attorney proudly bills 2,100 hours in 2002 and receives a bonus of $10,000, making her total compensation $135,000. She thus earned $64 per hour for billing 2,100 hours ($135,000/2,100 hours). The corporate attorney also exceeds the minimum billable hours and records a whopping 2,650 hours. He receives a bonus of $35,000, making his total compensation $160,000. Yet his hourly rate comes to just $60 per hour ($160,000/2,650 hours). For the extra 550 hours that he worked over the tax associate, he's only getting $45 an hour ($25,000/550).

Many attorneys find that once you reach your billable hours goal, any additional time spent to get bonus money just may not be worth it. As one East Coast tax attorney put it, "Why work the extra hours? Discretionary bonuses are always truly discretionary and in my experience they are rarely given. It's just not worth giving up your weekends for an extra $10,000 in life. That's why in my firm, 90 percent of the associates will have billable hours of 2,006 or 2,004, just enough to meet our 2,000 minimum billable hours requirement."

In addition to hefty bonuses, how do trips to the Caribbean, free dinners at exclusive restaurants, weekly massages and the latest technology gadgets like BlackBerrys, cells phones and laptops sound to you? These are just some of the many perks offered to associates by big law firms. As Fenwick & West's Allen Madison says, "Lawyers in law firms work hard, but they are rewarded for it. In fact, my firm sends associates who have billed a certain amount of hours to Hawaii every year for a one-week vacation, all travel expenses paid!"

Other common perks that may be provided by big law firms include the following:

- 401(k) plans – some firms also provide matching contributions

- Four to five weeks of vacation

- Health care plans

- Maternity leave – many firms provide three months of paid maternity leave

- Paternity leave – dads typically only get about a week

- Free parking and/or subsidized transportation – firms in large cities often help pay for commuting costs

- Domestic partner insurance coverage

- Health and dependent flexible spending accounts

- Childcare – firms often have contracts with local daycare centers to serve as backup to the child's normal daycare

- Sabbaticals are offered by some firms to senior associates (often up to six months)

- Mortgage assistance, usually for first-time home buyers

- Fitness club discounts

Getting down to work

The nature of the work tax attorneys perform differs depending on the city as well as on the firm. For example, in Washington D.C., many tax attorneys do policy work or controversy work because of the proximity of the IRS and Congress. In the South or the Northeast tax attorneys may tend to focus more on partnership work or closely held businesses. For large-scale corporate mergers and acquisitions there is perhaps no place like New York City. According to one tax attorney who has worked in both a smaller regional market and New York, "The tax work in New York is simply unparalleled. New York is fast-paced, intense and exciting. In my smaller regional market we worked on very good corporate transactional matters with many deals in the millions. In New York I work on deals that are in the billions everyday!"

Professor Boise, who formerly worked with a large New York law firm, agrees: "Because of the broad scope of economic activity in the city, New York law firms provide great experience and a great training ground. Experience in certain specialized areas of tax law, such as international tax or the taxation of financial products, is best obtained in New York, where international and financial markets activity is centered. Many people, like myself, spend their early years of practice with New York law firms and then take their experience to regional markets. It's a great way to set yourself apart in smaller markets."

But there can be a downside to working in such a fast-paced environment. Although big firm life can generally be hard on your personal life, in New York this is an even greater issue. A practicing tax attorney in New York warns those considering the Manhattan market, "You have to be willing to put up with a lot of personal sacrifices. You will easily miss vacations, holidays and other events with your significant other, friends and kids. Clients come to big New York law firms because we know how to get stuff done regardless of the time of year, day or night. If that means that you miss your best friend's wedding, then so be it."

Making partner

There is no fixed route or time frame for the path to partnership. At some law firms, it takes seven to eight years to become a partner. Other firms, particularly in New York, have longer partnership tracks, with attorneys working 10 years or more before joining the partnership ranks. The length of time may depend on exactly what is required to attain partner status. Obviously, an attorney must have proven that she is highly competent and has good substantive skills. But many firms also require that the attorney have a certain amount of client business, known as a book of business (for example, an attorney must have $250,000 in client business to make partner). For areas like tax where it may be difficult to develop a significant book of business, but where the attorney's expertise is required to assist lawyers in many other legal areas, some law firms consider the talents and individual contributions of the attorney in making partnership decisions. So the tax person who doesn't have a substantial book of business but serves as the technical expert on many of the firm's most significant corporate deals still has a shot at making partner.

Before you set your sights on making partner, however, know this. Gone are the days of making partner and then retiring to your office and playing golf every day while associates do all the work. Many partners are still fully engaged in practicing law and building their business. One associate observes, "Partners nowadays work hard and in some cases harder than they did as associates. Law firm competition is stiff and a partner can't afford to relax just because she has become a partner." The structure of law firm partnerships has also changed over the years. Many law firms now have a two-tier partnership structure for equity and non-equity partners. Equity partners, as owners, share in the profits of the law firm. These partners tend to have significant books of business and are often the most experienced attorneys. Non-equity partners don't share in the profits of the law firm and are compensated as regular employees. They are, however, allowed to use the title "partner" in their professional interactions. For some law firms, this non-equity status is viewed as training ground for junior partners (those who have practiced between 10 and 15 years) who are trying to build a book of business.

In addition to partnership status, many law firms offer positions as "of counsel." Historically, these positions were for senior partners who wanted to wind down their practice. They were also used for experienced attorneys lateraling to a new law firm, where the firm wanted to try out the relationship before offering the attorney full partnership. But in the past few years, of counsel positions have been used for another purpose, to give senior associates a title that reflects their expertise and may help them build a book of business.

The middlemen

Medium-sized and smaller law firms also offer great career paths for tax attorneys. The tax departments in these firms are usually smaller than those at large firms. Also, many of these firms are located in smaller cities or regional areas. Salaries at these firms depend on the local economy. Here's a random sample of four medium-sized firms in four different geographic regions:

Pacific Northwest: Miller Nash LLP, a 140-lawyer firm, has offices in Oregon and Washington. It has approximately 15 attorneys in its tax department. According to 2002 salary information available on FindLaw, first-year associates received base salaries of $85,000 and were required to bill a minimum of 1,750 billable hours.

Midwest: Ice Miller based in Indianapolis, with smaller offices in Chicago and Washington, D.C., has over 225 attorneys, with approximately 16 attorneys who specialize in tax. According to the FindLaw information for 2000, first-year associates received base salaries of $80,000 and were required to bill a minimum of 1,850 billable hours.

East Coast: Fox Rothschild LLP, a 250-lawyer firm with offices in Pennsylvania, New Jersey and Delaware, has approximately 20 attorneys in its tax department, many of whom practice in the estate planning area. It currently lists its starting salary for first-year associates at $90,000 and its minimum annual billable hour requirement as 1,800 to 1,900 hours.

South: Atlanta-based Smith, Gambrell & Russell, LLP, has over 185 lawyers. The firm's web site lists 16 attorneys in its tax department. According to FindLaw information for 2000, first-year associates received base salaries of $100,000 and were required to bill a minimum of 1,800 billable hours.

Tradeoffs

Salaries and bonuses at many mid-sized firms are lower than those at the largest firms. But the practice of law isn't all about money and prestige. What smaller and medium-sized law firms lack in financial rewards, they may more than make up for in level of responsibility and job security. Mid-sized and boutique firms may offer a young associate more hands-on training then she would normally get at a large law firm. Professor Boise worked in a mid-sized law firm after a stint in New York and notes, "With medium-size law firms you often get to do much of the very interesting work because you may be the only tax associate. For example, in medium-size or smaller firms that do complex partnership work and estate planning for owners of closely held businesses, the tax associate gets involved in almost every aspect of this work. At a large law firm, the clients tend to be big and very sophisticated, but the young tax associate may only do a very small piece of, say, a billion dollar merger or acquisition."

Melinda Merk, who worked at a small law firm before joining an accounting firm, agrees: "With smaller law firms, you get more hands-on experience. When I was an associate at a small firm, I had my own clients and was very involved in marketing and bringing in new business for the firm." According to an East Coast lawyer who used to practice with a large firm, "The advantage of a smaller regional firm is that you get to run the show and you run the deals."

Even though smaller or mid-size firms may offer associates more responsibility and client contact, they may not offer the same caliber of work or the vast resources that some tax attorneys want. According to a tax attorney in Washington, D.C., "The main disadvantage of working for a smaller organization was the resources. We simply did not have the same type of administrative or technical expertise as the larger firms."

The shingle hangers

Some tax attorneys decide to forgo the law firm life and hang their own shingle right in the middle of Small Town USA. These solo practitioners typically handle tax issues for individuals and small businesses. Although some may be able to specialize, particularly in estate tax planning or state tax law, others must serve as generalists – handling any tax issue that walks through the door. Many also do compliance work (fill out and file tax returns) or related legal work such as drafting contracts.

A range of work

Calvin Allen, a solo practitioner in Florida, decided to open his own tax firm after several years of practicing as a litigator. Discussing his work, he says, "Even though I have a tax practice and my client base is mostly interested in estate planning tax issues, I also do related, but nonetheless non-tax, work such as drafting trusts and wills. As a solo practitioner, I'm also often asked to do legal work that is completely unrelated to tax for my clients, like personal injury work or family issues like divorces. I refer a lot of that work to other attorneys."

Eve Borenstein, another tax attorney who decided to fly solo many years ago in Minneapolis, believes that it was the best professional decision she ever made. She explains, "The advantage of being a solo practitioner is that you are your own boss. You are the one who learns what is working or not about things like marketing and client relationships. You truly chart your own path. I love not having someone tell me what to do on these matters."

Although having prior tax experience is not required, many solo practitioners got their start in larger organizations. Borenstein began her tax career with a big accounting firm. "The years that I worked for one of the Big Eight, which is what they were at the time, were invaluable to helping me set up my own practice," she says. "I was able to get great experience and mentorship in tax law – something that would have been almost impossible to do directly out of law school on my own." Some single practitioners also have advanced degrees in taxation. Since solos lack the powerful marketing arms and brand-name recognition enjoyed by large law firms, these higher degrees are helpful in marketing their tax expertise to potential clients.

Profits all your own

For some solo practitioners the financial rewards can be just as great as, if not greater than, those offered by big law firms. Why? Because the profits earned by the solo practitioner are not shared with anyone. The amount a solo practitioner can expect to earn each year depends on factors such as the practitioner's location, tax specialty, experience level and networking ability. In general, solo lawyers practicing tax in major cities make a very nice living. Calvin Allen estimates that on average these attorneys may earn between $150,000 and $180,000 per year.

On the other hand, collecting these profits can be a burden most law firm associates, as employees, don't have to face. Calvin Allen complains, "Some days I spend more time on collecting fees than on actually practicing law." According to Eve Borenstein, "The administrative side of having my own practice is a lot more cumbersome. From billing to payroll, when you are a solo practitioner, you have to make sure everything is done. Even if you hire administrative help, you still have to supervise the work and you are required to get workman's compensation insurance, pay employment taxes and all of the other wonderful responsibilities that go along with being an employer."

Accounting Firms

Accounting firms offer an array of tax services often rivaling those offered by law firms – from mergers and acquisitions to tax compliance, VAT solutions and e-business services. Most tax lawyers who work for accounting firms work for one of the largest accounting firms. After the collapse of Arthur Anderson LLP, the "Final Four," as they are affectionately known, include Ernst & Young LLP, PricewaterhouseCoopers LLP, KPMG LLP and Deloitte & Touche LLP

Given the sheer size of these organizations which have offices throughout the world, it is often important for a tax lawyer working for one of the Big Four to become an expert in a particular niche. Lawyers in accounting firms are more likely to specialize in one tax area than attorneys at law firms. It is not uncommon for a tax lawyer working at an accounting firm to have clients across the country or even abroad. One accounting firm tax attorney says,

"The breadth of the work and the opportunities to work for sophisticated clients throughout the world is almost unparalleled by any organization, including the largest of the big law firms."

National office experts

Accounting firms are typically divided between a national tax office in Washington, D.C., and practice offices located throughout the United States and in many other countries. In the national office, tax attorneys tend to serve as technical experts on specialized areas and field questions from other accounting firm professionals in practice offices. These attorneys may work within a tax specialty and may even have a subspecialty based on their experience with specific issues. It is not uncommon to hear an attorney at the national office referred to as the Section "X" expert – meaning that she is an expert of that section of the Internal Revenue Code and any tax matters involving that section should be run by this expert. For example, the Houston office of one of the Big Four accounting firms may have a client with a complex debt restructuring (a company that needs to pay off some debt while borrowing from other sources to help improve the performance of its stock). The Houston office doesn't handle many debt restructurings so it calls the national office expert who deals with financial institutions and products, the group most experienced with these kinds of transactions.

Practice offices

The focus at the accounting firm's practice office differs from that at the national office. For one thing, tax attorneys in practice offices may not be experts in any particular tax specialty. Many of these attorneys work in broad practice areas, like corporate, state and local tax, or partnerships, and they are rarely experts on particular code sections. These attorneys are also more likely to deal directly with the client than the national office experts. In fact, a major part of their job is client development and managing the client relationship. Tax attorneys at practice offices may also do some compliance work. One lawyer even suggests that compliance work is a prerequisite for career success: "To succeed at an accounting firm you should go in and expect to do some compliance work. This is typically the type of person who will make partner."

In recent years, accounting firms have sought to expand their expertise by having experts located in various other offices outside the national office.

These national teams, as they are often called, offer tax experts within a particular subject area based somewhere other than Washington, D.C.

Hierarchical structure

Unlike law firms with two main classes of professionals, associate and partner, accounting firms have a very hierarchical structure, often including staff, supervising staff, managers, senior managers, directors and partners. Most tax attorneys start at either the supervising staff level or the manager level. It may take 10 to 12 years to reach partner status. Directorships at some accounting firms are reserved for those who will not become partners but are too senior and experienced to remain senior managers.

The work

So what exactly do tax attorneys at accounting firms do? Typical activities for tax attorneys at accounting firms might include:

- Tax planning projects for clients (goal: reduce client's tax burden)
- Sales of projects (sometimes referred to as products) to clients
- Research on current and future tax laws to search proactively for projects and products to sell to clients
- Writing memoranda on tax issues for clients or the firm
- Reviewing tax compliance and tax returns to find tax planning ideas and follow up on prior planning projects
- Management of client projects, including managing staff and other resources
- Advising clients (either reacting to requests or proactively contacting them) with regard to possible tax savings
- Networking to build a potential client pool

One attorney compares the work of a tax lawyer in an accounting firm to that of a law firm lawyer: "Work with accounting firms in my experience includes drafting opinion letters regarding the tax impact of a particular transaction or issue and tax technical memoranda. Also, we give oral tax advice with written documentation and we sit in on tax structuring discussions or planning work for our clients. Finally, we review large federal income tax returns. Having previously worked for a law firm, I think the tax return review work and the tax structuring discussions were the only accounting firm-specific type of work. Obviously, the tax structuring work exists at law firms, but it is generally reserved for more senior tax or corporate associates."

Walking a fine line

Picture this. You just advised your client on the tax law intricacies of a particular transaction with a third party. The client wants you to take the lead in drafting the purchase and sale agreement, but you work for an accounting firm. Can you draft this document?

Many tax attorneys at accounting firms will tell you that they can't and don't draft documents because to do so would be to engage in the unauthorized practice of law. The unauthorized practice of law rules that are adopted in some form by all 50 states provide that a non-lawyer corporation or entity can't employ attorneys to provide legal services to its customers. The purpose of these rules is to protect the public from receiving legal services by an unqualified person (i.e., one who has not met the state's qualifications for becoming a practicing attorney). Since the accounting firm is a non-lawyer entity, the attorneys it employs can't provide legal services.

Although providing tax services like advice and planning can in some ways be seen as providing legal services, many in the tax field agree that these activities are not prohibited under the unauthorized practice of law rules. This is because tax, unlike other areas of the law, contains a heavy overlap with accounting issues, so such services are not purely legal. Drafting documents and agreements, on the other hand, is considered a legal service. At least one tax attorney, however, is skeptical of the distinction: "The work is as close as you can get to drafting. Sure, the law firm will draft the document, but then we [the accounting firm] make the major substantive edits and changes to the document, so that when we are finished it is a completely different agreement. Would you call that drafting? Maybe yes, maybe no. It depends on whom you are asking."

The same unauthorized practice of law rules do not apply in other countries. Over the past decade, accounting firms have become some of the largest employers of lawyers and law firms in European countries. As an East Coast attorney notes, "It's a fine line between tax services and legal services, but there are many benefits to working in an accounting firm with this type of multidisciplinary team [of accountants and lawyers] and work environment." A multidisciplinary practice means that accounting firms can provide true one-stop shopping for its audit clients. In addition to performing the audit, they can handle global tax services and even legal services overseas. This was seen as an advantage by some organizations since as auditors, the accounting firm was already in a good position to understand the company and could easily be brought up to speed on other services that the organization was seeking.

Sarbanes-Oxley

But with new stricter rules under the Sarbanes-Oxley Act of 2002, the landscape for tax services and legal services provided by accounting firms overseas may change drastically. This legislation, enacted in July 2002 from bills sponsored by Sen. Paul Sarbanes, D-Md., and Rep. Michael Oxley, R-Ohio, is often referred to simply as Sarbanes-Oxley. As the government's response to the Enron scandal, the law is, among other things, designed to provide oversight of the accounting industry. Under Sarbanes-Oxley, accounting firms can't provide tax services to their audit clients without first getting approval from the corporation's audit committee.

One lawyer explains, "Before Sarbanes-Oxley, accounting firms sold their tax services to in-house tax departments, treasury departments, accounting departments and even the CFO. Oftentimes the in-house people were formerly employed by the accounting firm. It was like a friendly referral system. Now, with Sarbanes-Oxley, the friendship is over. Accountants who audit a client have to try and sell these other tax services to corporate audit committees who are made up by members of the company's board of directors and who often have no prior affiliation with the accounting firm. This could have a major impact on what tax work goes to the accounting firm and what work goes to a law firm or even a competitor accounting firm. The advantage of one-stop shopping is apparently not an advantage anymore."

Moreover, Sarbanes-Oxley also prohibits accounting firms from providing certain legal services to its audit clients. This could have a huge impact on accounting firms' legal services overseas. KPMG has discontinued providing full-scope legal services overseas and its associated legal network, KLegal International, has been disbanded. Other accounting firms with interests in overseas law firms are likely to follow. How this will affect the multidisciplinary and global services that accounting firms can provide remains to be seen. However, it is likely that some of this work will be picked up by law firms.

A range of salaries

Salaries at accounting firms vary widely. You'll find a good resource to benchmark salaries in TaxTalent.com's salary comparison tool. This service allows you to enter information about your current position or a desired position and then compare that against information in the database for similarly situated positions. "In general," according to TaxTalent.com's director, John O'Neill, "tax planners/consultants make more money, on the average, than do compliance people. Even though compliance is a vital part of the tax process, planning and consulting is where the big money savings is seen, and thus the rewards are greater for good work there. So many tax attorneys will do planning/consulting, but even here the differences in salary can be large." O'Neill adds, "With accounting firms it's all about leverage. For those coming from another organization like a law firm, you can negotiate a deal based on your past experience." Tax attorneys working at a firm's national office tend to make more than those in regional practice offices.

Corporations

Most major Fortune 500 companies have in-house tax departments. But don't be surprised that the ads for these jobs typically read "experienced only need apply." Entry-level, in-house positions are open to attorneys who have been practicing at least four or five years, with some jobs requiring 10 or more years of experience. Florida lawyer Wayne Hamilton notes, "There's less training in corporations, so they expect people to be experienced."

Working in-house

Many in-house tax attorneys are planners. Planners help develop tax techniques and strategies to minimize the corporation's effective tax rate. They often work closely with professionals in the company's finance and accounting departments to assess the impact of any tax strategies or plans on the corporation's financial statements. In-house counsel often work with outside law firms and accounting firms to develop and implement tax strategies or plans and they sometimes solicit formal opinions from these service providers on whether the desired tax treatment would likely be upheld if ever challenged by the IRS or a state taxing authority.

Some in-house tax attorneys also do controversy work. Controversy attorneys typically lead the company's state and/or federal tax audits. They deal directly with the IRS or a particular state tax agent during an audit. They also handle the matters on appeal to an administrative agency or during litigation in a court proceeding. Like planners, they often work with attorneys at law firms and experts at accounting firms to address controversy issues. In-house counsel Wayne Hamilton describes this relationship: "I work closely with outside counsel in developing my company's response to an audit issue. In that regard, I'm like a project manager who coordinates with the law firm and manages the issue with the IRS." Pete Lowy, a controversy tax attorney with a large corporation, says, "In my current position, I handle federal and state tax disputes on both the administrative and judicial levels, and with respect to many different kinds of taxes – federal and state income taxes, franchise taxes, sales and use taxes, and motor fuels taxes."

Of course, many in-house tax attorneys do a little bit of everything – planning, controversy and compliance. For example, Randle Pollard, domestic tax counsel for a large pharmaceutical company, outlines his responsibilities: "I provide a variety of legal services for my company. I represent my company's private foundations. I also provide legal advice to our state and local tax compliance department and legal assistance on our federal audit. Then I help out on federal tax issues in general – more of a planning role. Finally, I do some state lobbying on tax-related matters."

In many companies, tax attorneys specialize in one area. For example, a typical in-house tax department will have a vice president of taxes who usually reports to a CFO. Under the vice president is a planning department that may be divided among international planners, domestic planners and state and local tax planners. There will also likely be an audit and controversy group, which may have attorneys who handle federal and state tax audits and manage these issues through the appeals process and any court proceedings. Lastly, there will be a compliance section in charge of preparing the company's tax returns. This compliance section may have divisions for international, domestic, and state and local compliance. In addition to attorneys, other professionals in the tax department include accountants (mostly CPAs), particularly in the compliance section. Most tax attorneys work in the planning division or the controversy section.

In a smaller company, as Wayne Hamilton notes, there may only be a few tax professionals, so the lines between planning, controversy and compliance blur. "In a smaller corporation you have to handle more issues because you may be the only tax attorney. You become like a generalist."

The sky's the limit

Salary information for tax in-house positions is a lot harder to track than that for attorneys at law and accounting firms. TaxTalent.com's job listing service includes some corporate positions, and FindLaw's web site is another good source for listings of in-house tax positions. You might even find this information on general job search boards like Monster.com.

Many in-house tax experts will tell you that their salary is comparable to those in big law firms and accounting firms when you take into account all of the perks and benefits. For these in-house experts, compensation is more than just the base salary. It can also include stock options, 401(k) matching plans, employee stock option plans, company cars, on-site daycare and bonuses tied into management and corporate performance. These bonuses can be very large – sometimes 40 to 50 percent of the professional's base salary. "When you add it all up," observes Hamilton, "a base salary can easily go up by $50,000 or $100,000 dollars from bonuses, and when the stock market is doing really good, the sky is the limit."

Nonprofit corporations

Those less driven by profit than by a desire to do good might consider going in-house with a nonprofit organization. In addition to for-profit corporations, some tax lawyers take in-house positions with nonprofit corporations. These tax attorneys generally help the nonprofits abide with the many tax laws governing them. Lawyers implement programs, policies and procedures and help in the management of the organization. In this respect, they are more like business people than pure attorneys.

Most of these nonprofits are large organizations like universities, hospitals or private foundations. In-house tax experts typically specialize on particular tax issues that apply to their organization. For example, a tax attorney working for a university might specialize in gift and estate tax issues as she designs and implements giving programs for prospective donors to the university. A tax attorney with a large private foundation may focus more on exempt organization tax rules that specifically affect the operations of private foundations, such as whether the foundation is subject to certain excise taxes. Other tax attorneys work for smaller organizations where they handle more policy work and may even engage in a fair amount of non-legal work. Many think-tank organizations or trade associations hire such tax attorneys.

As with for-profit corporations, tax attorneys at nonprofit corporations often have several years of experience before going in-house. Many have worked for the IRS or accounting firms. Salaries at nonprofit organizations tend to be lower than those at law firms, accounting firms and large corporations; many positions start at less than $100,000. The *Chronicle of Philanthropy* runs a free, nonprofit job search service on its web site (www.philanthropy.com) which is searchable by location and type of job.

If nonprofit compensation is lower than that at for-profit organizations, the practical experience and other rewards can still be great. John Pomeranz, a tax attorney with the Alliance for Justice (a national association of environmental, civil rights, mental health, women's, children's and consumer advocacy organizations), observes that "nonprofits are a wonderful place to hone in on your tax skills while helping a charity and the public at the same time."

Government

According to the 1998 IRS Data Book, the IRS employs some 97,000 people and takes on an extra 74,000 volunteers during the tax-filing season. Another 24,000 tax professionals work for various federal agencies. Although these tax professionals come from a variety of backgrounds and include accountants, actuaries and economists, many are also tax lawyers. In fact, Uncle Sam is probably the largest employer of tax attorneys.

Why do so many attorneys choose government service? Besides the sheer number of jobs that are available, many attorneys believe that the training offered by the government is unbeatable. According to Florida lawyer Wayne Hamilton, "Prior government service is very helpful for private industry. It gives you a chance to receive excellent training and can prepare you for numerous tax positions that you would not have been able to get straight out of law school. In my case, after several years with the IRS, I landed a tax attorney position with a Fortune 10 company."

IRS advantages

Of all the government agencies, the IRS is by far the largest employer of tax lawyers. Training, training and more training is perhaps the biggest advantage of working for the IRS. Shelia Dansby Harvey, a tax attorney with the Internal Revenue Service in Houston, explains, "The IRS offers excellent training. We regularly have training programs taught by top experts in the tax field. For example, we recently had high-level, cutting-edge courses on corporate reorganizations, partnerships, financial accounting and international tax issues. All of these courses were taught by top experts in the field from New York University. Also, for new tax lawyers, the IRS offers numerous training programs on the basics of a particular specialty. For example, there is a tax litigation school that lasts for approximately one week where these lawyers learn the basics of tax practice and procedure and do mock trials so that they can get comfortable with practicing before Tax Court."

In addition to training, IRS attorneys enjoy a fair amount of responsibility – after all, they are often shaping the laws and policies that govern taxpayers' lives. As Harvey observes, "You have a lot more responsibility in government services than with law firms because you are the decision maker. You aren't just researching a small issue in the big puzzle, and you get this responsibility early on – often in your first year of practice." For those nervous about being thrown into the deep end right away, she adds, "You also get an excellent safety net, so when you are new and get all this responsibility there is a system of checks and balances that helps ensure that you won't make harmful mistakes. This strong support system allows the young attorney to take on a huge level of responsibility, while at the same [time receiving] the right amount of supervision."

Wayne Hamilton agrees. "With the IRS," he says, "you will probably have the fastest learning curve, because they are not hesitant to give you an issue with a lot of responsibility. Thus, the quantity and quality of work comes much quicker than in the private sector. You can get a lot of exposure and you don't have to worry about paying your dues so much."

Another benefit of government service, says Harvey, is that "you are not pressured about getting a certain outcome. Instead, you must focus on getting to the right answer – not the answer that your client wants to hear." Lilo Hester, a former IRS employee, voices a similar opinion: "With the government you are trying to get the right answer. In the private sector you just have to have a right answer. Also, in the government I got to effect change. If the rule is not right, you can open a new project and change the rule to the right answer. However, in the private sector all you can do is influence change."

National versus field offices

So what do IRS attorneys do? That depends on where they work. In the IRS National Office in Washington, D.C., attorneys are divided into substantive areas such as corporate, income tax and accounting and employee benefits. Within these areas, different branches may cover specific code sections.

Much like the tax lawyers in the national offices of accounting firms, the IRS National Office attorneys are true experts in a particular area of law.

Lisa Tavares, a former attorney with the IRS National Office, outlines her responsibilities: "I was in the litigation branch of the IRS National Office. We reviewed Tax Court briefs and memoranda and assisted the Department of Justice Tax Division in handling cases that were appealed. Because many of the Tax Division attorneys are generalists, we served as their experts in a particular area. Also, we drafted IRS guidance like field service advice and technical advice memoranda. We sometimes received congressional inquiries about a policy or regulation – things like 'My constituent didn't like x or y.' So we prepared written responses to congressmen or senators. My branch also worked closely with attorneys from the Treasury Department on regulations and policy statements."

Other attorneys work in IRS field offices, where the emphasis is more on specific situations than on general statements of policy or expertise in one area of tax law. Wayne Hamilton, who used to work in an IRS field office, explains: "There are several differences between the IRS National Office and the IRS field offices. The IRS National Office deals a lot with ruling requests by taxpayers and thus attorneys here need to have an in-depth knowledge of a particular area. Conversely, in an IRS field office, the attorneys must handle a potpourri of issues, which depend on what is going on with the taxpayers in their area. Also, the IRS National Office's focus is consistency among taxpayers – how does this impact taxpayers across the country? The IRS field offices look to see if a particular taxpayer is in compliance with the tax law. A field office in Miami may not be concerned with what a field office in Ohio is doing. Lastly, the workload is different between the National Office and the field office. In the field office you are actually on the front line, handling numerous issues. You also have more autonomy in the decision-making process and quicker response times."

Shelia Dansby Harvey, who works in the IRS's Houston office, advises attorneys to consider their goals and interests before targeting a particular office. "If you want to be a litigator," she says, "you should go to the IRS field office. Also, if you need variety in your work you should also go to the IRS field office. But if you want to master a particular area in tax, you should go to the IRS National Office. Also, if you are more of a researcher and writer, the IRS National Office may be better for you."

IRS tax attorneys in the National Office work closely with tax attorneys at the Treasury Department. Much of this interaction takes place when drafting tax regulations. Lilo Hester, a former National Office attorney, believes that the

National Office offers valuable experience: "Working at the IRS National Office or Treasury is an excellent place to improve writing skills and to get a hands-on understanding of how tax policy is developed, interpreted and applied." The expertise gained at the IRS can later translate into a high-level position in the private sector, as Hester can attest. She was the principal drafter of the Section 1441 tax regulations, which deal with certain withholding tax rules, and is now a partner in the national office of Ernst & Young LLP.

The Tax Division

IRS tax attorneys may also interact with attorneys from the U.S. Department of Justice, Tax Division, commonly referred to as the Tax Division. The Tax Division has more than 350 attorneys in 14 civil, criminal and appellate trial sections, most based in Washington, D.C., who represent the United States and its officers in civil and criminal litigation related to internal revenue laws. The Tax Division is led by an assistant attorney general, who is appointed by the president and confirmed by the Senate. Tax Division civil attorneys litigate on behalf of the federal government in federal district courts, bankruptcy courts and state courts. Prosecutors from the criminal enforcement section investigate and prosecute complex financial crimes. Appellate sections handle civil and criminal appeals.

Civil service salaries

As with most federal government positions, your salary depends on your civil service level (typically represented by a "GS" and then a number) and your location. Those straight out of law school may start at a GS-11 level and earn a little over $50,000 per year. Within three to four years this attorney can expect to make $30,000 to $40,000 more than his starting salary. Government salaries for attorneys with some experience may start at the GS-13 level (approximately $75,000 to $82,000) or the GS-14 level, which is capped at approximately $92,000. Depending on the government agency and the individual attorney, it is possible to start at the GS-15 level, which is capped at approximately $114,000.

In addition to base salaries, the government has a defined-benefit retirement plan and retirement savings deferred compensation plan. The government makes certain matching contributions to these plans so that the total compensation package may include your base salary plus 15 percent of your base. The Department of Justice provides the following salary ranges on its web site:

GS-12 ($58,070-$75,492)
GS-13 ($69,054-$89,774)
GS-14 ($81,602-$106,806)
GS-15 ($95,987-$124,783)

Tax Court clerkships

Eighteen regular judges and ten special trial judges sit on the U.S. Tax Court. Most of these judges have law clerks. Most clerkships are two-year positions. There are approximately 20 to 25 positions open annually. Tax Court clerkships are considered very prestigious in the tax world. Many people apply for clerkships, but only a few are chosen. The experience gained by being on the cutting edge of tax law as it is being made, dissected and modified is hard to match in most tax positions. Because clerks generally draft legal opinions for the cases before their judges, research and writing skills are critical.

Barbara Pierson Roy, a former clerk with Judge Stanley J. Goldberg, reflects on the value of her clerkship experience: "My experience at the Tax Court helped me understand how the tax law system works. The court hears cases involving a wide variety of tax issues, so it helps you if you haven't determined what particular area of tax law on which you want to focus." Mildeen Worrell, a tax attorney for the House Ways and Means Committee, adds that working with a judge can provide young lawyers with strong mentors. "My clerkship was truly an awesome experience," she says. "A majority of my time was spent analyzing tax law and writing concise opinions; this experience allowed me to develop great confidence in my ability to become a good tax lawyer. I clerked for the Hon. Judge Joel Gerber who spent a lot of one-on-one mentoring time with me. For every opinion I drafted, he spent time with me, often playing the role of devil's advocate and arguing the opposing side. This type of mentoring, tutoring and constant feedback is crucial for beginning lawyers."

"You are given a great deal of independence and autonomy in your work as a Tax Court clerk," observes another former clerk, "much more than my friends at law firms who only work on a small piece of an issue. Thus, once you leave the clerkship you have an advantage over other attorneys with the same years of experience." If you know you want to do transactional work like corporate mergers and acquisitions, a Tax Court clerkship may not be for you.

But Allen Madison, a former clerk for Judge Lawrence Whalen, thinks that even transactional attorneys will learn something from a clerkship. "Although Tax Court clerkships may not be viewed as prestigious in the transactional deal world," he says, "I found my clerkship very helpful because I still got to know about these sophisticated corporate tax deals. They were often attacked by the IRS, which meant the issue wound up in the Tax Court and we got to really dissect them."

Clerks make approximately $3,300 to $4,500 a month. If their salaries are not as high as their peers at law or accounting firms, their hours are generally much more reasonable. One former clerk calls it "a more 9-to-5 type of job." Tax Court clerkships are, however, very difficult to land straight out of law school. Most clerks have LL.Ms.

Working on the Hill

Tax lawyers also serve as experts to congressional committees. These tax attorneys, sometime referred to as Hill attorneys, work directly for one of the three major tax-writing committees: the House Committee on Ways and Means, the Senate Finance Committee and the Joint Committee on Taxation.

Committees

The House Committee on Ways and Means was created in 1789 and is the oldest standing committee in Congress. It is charged with oversight of legislation, methods and means of raising revenue for the government, economic policy, international trade, welfare, Social Security, Medicare and healthcare policy. It is the main committee responsible for writing tax legislation.

The Senate Finance Committee has jurisdiction over a number of matters including tax, Social Security, Medicare, Supplemental Security Income, Medicaid, family welfare programs, social services, unemployment compensation, maternal and child health, revenue sharing, tariff and trade legislation, and public debt.

Finally, the Joint Committee on Taxation, or JCT, is closely involved in every aspect of the tax legislative process. It prepares hearing pamphlets, committee reports and conference reports (statements of managers); assists the Office of Legislative Counsel in the drafting of statutory language; assists members of Congress with the development and analysis of legislative proposals; assists members of Congress in addressing constituent issues and problems; prepares revenue estimates of all revenue legislation considered by the Congress; reviews large proposed income tax refunds; and initiates investigations of various aspects of the federal tax system.

Members of Congress

Some senators and representatives, typically those who sit on one of the tax-writing committees, have tax lawyers on their staff. Unlike the tax attorneys who work for the committees, these lawyers, known as tax legislative assistants, deal with tax rules and policies that affect the particular congressperson's constituency. They also work on other issues besides taxation. As Mildeen Worrell, a tax attorney for the House Committee on Ways and Means, explains, "Very often, a tax legislative assistant will cover additional areas of responsibility under the committee's jurisdiction such as trade or healthcare. If one is willing to expand into these areas, these positions exist both on the Democratic side as well as the Republican side."

The work, the hours and the pay

So what do Hill attorneys do every day? According to Worrell, "As an attorney for a tax-writing committee I spend a lot of time drafting tax laws, managing committee consideration of tax legislation, preparing for and conducting hearings on major tax issues or specific legislative proposals, conducting briefing sessions for legislative assistants of the committee members, responding to a member's tax questions, reading articles and any other relevant information on major tax issues or proposed legislation, preparing materials for 'floor' debate of tax legislation, participating in reconciling different tax measures as passed by the House and the Senate – i.e., conference report (this is ultimately signed into law) – drafting memoranda to members, and preparing response letters to constituents' inquiries."

Writing skills are crucial for Hill attorneys. "If your goal is to work on Capitol Hill," says Worrell, "you must like both policy analysis and writing. Great analytical skills also are necessary because you must constantly evaluate the pros and cons of proposed legislation and the impact the legislation will have on the population (for example, is it skewed to the wealthy? Does it accomplish the intended goal? Are there hidden unintended consequences? Can the law be manipulated? Who will take advantage of the law?). If you like certainty and bright guidelines, then working on the Hill is probably not the place for you because you often realize that a lot of rules must be written with some level of flexibility in order to accomplish the intended goal. This may create some 'gray areas.' In addition, it is often necessary to develop legislation that would modify existing rules in order to stop abuses."

Hill attorneys work closely with economists, actuaries and statisticians. They also must attend many meetings – so many in fact that they may not get to actually writing and doing their "day job" until late in the evening. However, during congressional recesses, their work hours are closer to 9 to 5.

Salaries vary among Hill attorneys. Since most are experienced and have practiced with law firms, accounting firms or other government agencies, their salaries reflect this experience and many start at the GS-13 level or higher, with salaries close to $100,000. In addition to providing comfortable compensation and challenging experience, working on the Hill may lead to opportunities in the private sector. Because Hill attorneys are at the cutting edge of new tax laws and policies, they are highly sought after by private firms.

State government

The federal government is not the only governmental employer of tax lawyers. For those interested in state tax law, government positions at state agencies can offer useful training grounds. Most state departments of revenue or taxation and state legislative committees dealing with tax legislation have tax legal positions. Many of these positions are in controversy, where the state tax attorney serves as an auditor or hearing officer. Other positions are policy-oriented or legislative in nature, much like the Hill attorneys discussed above.

Whatever the position, a state tax attorney can form indispensable relationships with government officials and gain a thorough understanding of the state's position on various issues. This insight is often invaluable for those attorneys who leave state government to work in the private sector, often at accounting firms. In general, both the hours and the pay for state tax attorneys are less than those found in federal government positions or the private sector.

Academia

If analyzing policy and speaking before large crowds is your thing, you might consider a teaching career. "This career path is really for people who like the theoretical challenge of tax law and also like the challenge of explaining it to others," says Craig Boise, a tax professor at Case Law School in Cleveland.

Most tax professors join the faculty after a few years of practice, although some start right out of law school or an LL.M program. Law schools do not generally publish salaries for tax professors; many beginning professors can earn around $100,000, while those working for private universities earn more. While these figures may not compete with big law firm salaries, they're not bad for professionals who don't work year-round and get many vacations and breaks.

In fact, it is this lifestyle that makes teaching tax such an attractive career. Many professors teach just one or two classes a semester and hold office hours on their off days. Some professors also serve as consultants or outside counsels at law or accounting firms and thereby supplement their income by working part time for private industry. But before you assume that teaching tax is a leisurely job, remember that even if they don't work year-round, tax professors spend a lot of time reviewing current tax policy, cases and regulations. This translates into hours and hours of class preparation. Tax professors are also expected to publish articles or books on a frequent basis. So, much of that "free time" outside the classroom is actually devoted to researching and writing articles, periodicals and/or treatises.

Get the BUZZ on Top Schools

Read what STUDENTS and ALUMNI have to say about:

- Admissions
- Academics
- Career Opportunities
- Quality of Life
- Social Life

Surveys on thousands of top programs
College • MBA • Law School • Grad School

VAULT
> the most trusted name in career information™

Go to www.vault.com

Employer FAQs

CHAPTER 6

Knowing what it's like to work for a particular organization is just the first step in mapping your career in the tax field. Other issues to consider when narrowing your choices include how much that first job really matters, the pros and cons of switching between organizations, combining parenthood with a tax law career, diversity in the tax profession and pro bono opportunities.

Your First Tax Position

You'll never forget your first job as a tax lawyer – although you might wish you could. That first position can be very important to determining the rest of your career. Some attorneys will stay with the same organization throughout their careers. Others may switch jobs three, four or even five times. Tony Santiago, president of the recruiting firm TaxSearch, advises lawyers, "That first tax position really matters. If you don't start at a big law firm, big accounting firm or key government position, you will always have to explain why you didn't."

According to several tax professionals, it's not so much what your first legal position is, but instead how much prestige it carries. This is certainly the case with those who take certain non-traditional tax positions. For example, prestigious court clerkships, although not tax-specific, can help you hone your writing skills – skills that any employer will find highly desirable. Moreover, because clerkships only last a year or two, they will not put you far behind your former classmates who headed straight for a tax job. Professor Boise, a former clerk on the U.S. Court of Appeals for the Eighth Circuit, urges candidates to consider a clerkship: "You'll get to practice law for the rest your life, but you generally have only a small window of time to do a clerkship."

Law firm first?

Many practitioners believe that if you start your career at a law firm, it will be easier to transfer to an accounting firm or a corporation than vice versa. Top-tier law firms believe that the training provided by an accounting firm or a corporation is not as rigorous as their own. Melinda Merk, who works for a top accounting firm, says that "law firm experience can be very helpful before going to another organization like an accounting firm. It will provide you with a great basic legal foundation and a 'big picture' on how planning works. It will also help to develop your drafting and legal writing skills."

It may be difficult to get this law firm experience later on in your career. According to Professor Boise, "It is generally easier to get law firm experience at the beginning of your career rather than trying to switch to a law firm after having worked in-house, for example, or for an accounting firm." In fact, it is also possible that you may not get credit for your years of experience if you switch, or "lateral," to a law firm years later.

For example, assume Jane Taxpert starts in the tax department of a major law firm directly out of law school. By 2003, she has been practicing at this firm for six years. Assume her classmate Jim Taxwannabee starts his career at an accounting firm. After six years, he lands a job at Jane's law firm. Jane is now a sixth-year associate, but Jim lost a few years in his lateral move and is considered a fourth-year associate. As recruiter Tony Santiago explains, "Unless he is coming from Treasury, Capital Hill, the IRS National Office or similar positions where he can leverage his political ties or expertise on regulations or tax rulings, the weight of his experience will not be as valued as Jane's time at the law firm."

Many tax professionals agree that government experience can replace law firm training for people transitioning out of the Internal Revenue Service or the Treasury Department. A law firm may choose to hire such tax professionals for their expertise in a particular area of tax law or because they have helped write specific regulations or rulings.

This emphasis on law firm training may be shifting, however. "We are beginning to see people switch more easily between these organizations," reports John O'Neill. "Although it may be a little more difficult to go from, say, an accounting firm to a top-tier law firm, we aren't seeing that many people who have problems switching to smaller firms. Of course, this all depends on your law school and your class ranking, but good tax people do not hurt for finding quality tax jobs. These are the ones with the 'whole package' – those who are business-minded, have good communication skills and a high work ethic, keep up with trends, go to good schools, get good grades, have friendly and outgoing personalities, dress professionally. These people will always have a good job, no matter where they start."

Making the Switch

For those already practicing in the tax field, there often comes a time when the grass looks greener elsewhere. Whether you are at a law firm and want to move to an accounting firm or at an accounting firm and interested in a corporation, switching employers has become very common. Richard Larkins, a partner at Ernst & Young, notes, "There are all sorts of routes to the top. Some people at my level started at a big law firm, while others started at the IRS. Many have switched jobs two or three times before finally becoming partners. The point is to figure out what you want out of your professional life and pick those positions best suited to meet your needs. This may require moving around or you may be fortunate and be able to stay with the same organization. There is simply no one way to get to the top."

Before switching to a new organization it is important to consider some of the advantages and disadvantages in working within the new environment. In this regard, TaxTalent.com sponsors a career forum on its web site that offers career coaching for those considering switching positions as well as articles on such issues as the counteroffer, who should and should not look for a new job, and whether someone should remain in their current position. The following is a brief overview of some factors you may wish to consider.

Law firm practice

Training can't be beat

Law firms provide some of the best training grounds available for tax attorneys. Many people who have gone on to work at other organizations got their start at a law firm. Mildeen Worrell, tax counsel for the House Ways and Means Committee, found her law firm experience to be invaluable, explaining, "Law firms give you fundamental training and credibility in other organizations. I practiced for a few years at a major law firm before going on the Hill. This training helped me to be an overall well-rounded tax attorney. In addition to the legal training, research and writing fundamentals, law firms provide the opportunity to learn the so-called 'soft skills,' those interpersonal skills that are necessary to effectively navigate your path in an organization – especially in a world where politics are a way of life such as on the Hill."

TaxTalent.com's John O'Neill highlights other advantages of working in a law firm environment, including the opportunity to improve writing skills, develop better legal research skills, increase thinking and communicating from a legal perspective, work on different types of projects (like transactions, audit defense, litigation, contracts), and work almost exclusively with other attorneys. Moreover, some corporations like to hire tax attorneys with specific law firm experience.

Long hours and limited choices

So what do lawyers consider the disadvantages of working in a law firm? Hours, hours and more hours! Working too many hours is a common complaint for law firm associates, especially at the bigger firms. A tax lawyer in the Midwest who switched from a law firm to a corporation, explains, "I just couldn't handle the hours anymore. My wife and I want to start a family and I can't see spending so much time at work and hardly any time raising my kids. Even though I worked less hours as a tax lawyer than the corporate associates at my law firm, it was still too much time." Many lawyers at large law firms work an average of 10 to 12 hours a day with only seven or eight of those spent on billable matters. Associates typically only get credit for bonus and promotion purposes for the amount of billable hours they work. Pro bono activities, writing articles and attending CLE courses and handling other administrative firm work, albeit necessary, often competes with the attorney's "free time." Some law firms have tried to minimize this impact by counting some of the time spent on these non-billable activities toward the attorney's yearly billable goals. Still, "billable time is still the most important time," says an East Coast lawyer. "After all, the law firms are for-profit entities."

For solo practitioners or those at smaller law firms, the drawbacks include burdensome administrative issues, like collecting fees from clients. Calvin Allen, a solo practitioner in Key West, Fla., says, "I spend a lot of time preparing client bills and collecting amounts owed for my services. In many cases, I have to negotiate up-front retainers to ensure that I will actually get paid for my services."

Another complaint from some tax attorneys is that you can't truly specialize in one tax area at a law firm. Of course, there are exceptions for certain practice areas like estate planning, international tax, exempt organizations, employee benefits, and state and local tax. And there are some law firms known for expertise in a certain kind of tax. But many tax departments at big law firms handle a range of tax issues. What this means for the tax associate is that she is at the mercy of the firm as to what tax experience she will gain. One lawyer practicing on the East Coast finds that "in law firms you are more vulnerable to what clients come in the door. I learned this the hard way when I practiced with one of largest law firms in the country (in the top five in terms of size). When I came out of school, I said I only wanted to do international tax. But when I got to the law firm it seems as if I did everything but international tax."

Moreover, the economy can affect the nature of a law firm's tax practice. Some tax departments have few, if any, of their own clients and instead rely on referrals from corporate lawyers. In the heyday of the dot-com craze many tax departments thrived from the work generated by their corporate colleagues. But as the stock market dried up, so did the work. Those firms that depended on high-tech deals were hit the hardest and the last few years have seen massive layoffs, including for tax attorneys. Some firms, including Silicon Valley's Brobeck, Phleger & Harrison LLP, folded altogether.

Accounting firms

Sophisticated clients and opportunities to specialize

Accounting firms also offer good training for the tax professional. One of the main advantages of working for a big accounting firm is the exposure to sophisticated clients and transactions. Large accounting firms have offices around the world and offer truly global operations – something that only a few large law firms can claim. Moreover, accounting firms often work on the best and biggest transactions. One of the reasons may simply be that there are only four big accounting firms left, so there are enough great projects to be spread among them. But John O'Neill suggests another reason: "Accounting firms get some of the best work because they are tremendous at marketing themselves."

Accounting firms also offer the opportunity to specialize. This allows a tax lawyer to become an expert in a narrow area more quickly than a law firm associate whose time is spread thinly over many different tax specialties. Since accounting firms are located in every major city and most major locations throughout the world, there are opportunities to work just about anywhere. This is especially helpful for two-wage-earner families – if your spouse works for an accounting firm, he can be very flexible in changing job locations while staying gainfully employed with one organization.

Compliance rather than controversy

On the other hand, the nature of the work may not appeal to all tax lawyers. Attorneys at accounting firms may be expected to do some level of compliance work. An attorney in the Northeast warns, "If you are going to work for an accounting firm, you need to consider how much compliance work you will have to do and what the nature of the compliance will be." For some attorneys this compliance work may mean just reviewing tax returns. But others might have to prepare corporate tax returns for a group of corporations. The same attorney adds, "even if you are just reviewing tax returns, it's still difficult because perhaps you have never prepared this return. How do you supervise someone on a return if you have never done one yourself?"

Another consideration for tax professionals is the limitation on legal services accounting firm lawyers may provide. Attorneys at accounting firms cannot litigate or draft legal documents. So if you are interested in writing briefs or drafting agreements, an accounting firm may not be the best environment for you.

Corporations

A better balance

People choose the in-house route for a variety of reasons – for a more balanced lifestyle, exposure to business concerns, or greater authority and independence. According to Wayne Hamilton, who works in-house for a corporation in Florida, "The corporate lifestyle can't be beat. I still work hard but nowhere nearly as many hours as at a big law firm or accounting firm." Randle Pollard, a tax attorney at a large pharmaceutical company, says he chose an in-house position "because of the flexibility to evolve into a business person and get challenging work at competitive pay as compared to a law firm or accounting firm practice." Pete Lowy, a controversy tax attorney with a large corporation, explains his choice: "I went in-house because it provided me with a level of responsibility and control over my work that I did not see myself getting in a traditional law practice."

Just one client

A disadvantage cited by some in-house counsel is the lack of diversity in their work. Unlike attorneys at a law firm or an accounting firm, an in-house lawyer works for just one client. Some attorneys might find this boring. Career advancement also tends to be much slower in a corporation than in a law or accounting firm. According to one in-house lawyer, "You have to wait for someone to die before you can get a promotion around here." Some attorneys complain that it is hard to leave a corporate position and return to a law firm or an accounting firm – in other words, once you are there, you may be stuck. But John O'Neill disagrees. "It is no longer the case that tax lawyers in corporations can't switch positions," he says. "We are seeing folks go to law firms and accounting firms with their corporate experience being looked at as an asset."

Most corporate tax jobs are only available to those who have been practicing in the field for several years and who have law firm or accounting firm experience. But some corporations may hire former government employees when their specific expertise is needed. This is most common with controversy positions and in the state and local tax area. For example, a corporation with significant operations in the state of Virginia might hire someone who was formerly an agent or hearing officer with the Virginia Department of Revenue.

Other factors to consider

Making the switch to a corporation can be a big step for someone with a law firm or accounting firm background. No longer will you practice among a group of your lawyer peers. Now your peers will be based on levels and will include many different kinds of professionals, like accountants, managers, engineers and even scientists. John O'Neill suggests that "when considering a position in the tax department, you should consider the following questions:

- Is the tax department proactive in its thinking and working?

- Is the tax department held in high esteem within the company?

- Is there a track for someone with your background to make moves into more responsible roles? (For example, if you are an attorney and only accountants are in management positions, it might not be a good match.)

- Can you do the type of work you like to do?

- Will your work have the impact you are looking for within the organization?"

The IRS

There's only one

Government positions, especially those with the IRS, can offer excellent training for tax attorneys. In fact, when you look at the backgrounds of some of the leading tax experts, they have prior government service somewhere on their resume. Like accounting firms, the IRS (particularly in the National Office) offers the opportunity to specialize and become an expert in a particular area. Also, the IRS can offer a more balanced lifestyle than a law firm. "It's much easier to have a true 40-hour week at the IRS," says a lawyer in the Midwest. Finally, the sheer number of sophisticated issues and transactions reviewed by the IRS cannot be equaled by any organization. As one tax attorney observes, "There are thousands of law firms and accounting firms out there working on deals, coming up with plans and aggressively fighting for their clients. But there is only one IRS who gets to see all of this."

Government bureaucracy

Although many practitioners have found their IRS experiences very positive, one disadvantage commonly cited is that the bureaucracy of the organization can lead to people feeling pigeonholed. One former IRS attorney says, "It's so easy to get stuck in your position at the IRS, with promotions just one level up taking five or even ten years. Part of the problem is that once you are known for being a good worker – perhaps you have helped draft good regulations in an area or have otherwise developed a name for yourself as the 'go to' person on a particular issue or area – it's not cost effective to move you to a new area."

Exploring non-tax options

It's not uncommon for a tax lawyer to launch herself on one career path and then change midway to try another field outside tax law. Wayne Hamilton, now an associate counsel with a major automotive company, describes his departure from the tax world: "I started as a tax lawyer working for the IRS and received excellent training. Several years later, I switched over into private industry – a Fortune 10 company at the time. I'm now embarking on my third career path as a lawyer outside the tax department, working on general legal issues that affect my company. I could not have made this move without having proven myself as a solid tax professional."

Many lawyers believe that it is easier to switch from tax law to other legal specialties like corporate law or litigation than the other way around. Allen Madison, who works for Fenwick & West, explains, "I don't think it is easy for corporate or litigation lawyers to switch to tax. Generally, the issues that tax attorneys face are much more complex from both a factual and legal perspective. I would think the person switching would become overwhelmed rather quickly. My guess is that switching from tax to corporate and litigation would be easier because the issues are more simplistic from a factual and legal perspective. My understanding, however, is that in corporate law there is a hierarchy that doesn't exist as much in tax. This may be unnerving to the unprepared tax lawyer making the switch."

Other tax attorneys leave the law altogether. Some CFOs, treasurers and other business leaders got their start as tax lawyers. John O'Neill of TaxTalent.com confirms that he sees this all the time as a recruiter and adds, "The beauty of having a solid tax background is that it gives you the ability to change. Having this background often gives you an edge over other business types which is why it's not uncommon that some of the best business people have their roots in tax."

Working Moms

According to *Working Mother* magazine, there are 26 million working mothers in the United States. They hold positions in all kinds of organizations, from large multinational companies to one- or two-man shops. Many employers are trying to make it easier for working parents to have productive careers while also having family lives. Some organizations offer part-time positions and on-site daycare facilities, while others offer flex-time, telecommuting and other aids for the working parent.

Many lawyers agree that being a working mom and juggling a productive professional life is difficult no matter where you work. Corporations and government positions can be more flexible, but the cost of this flexibility might be a more stagnant career. According to one attorney who worked for an accounting firm, "In my experience, being a working mom was a serious struggle and I think it's hard to make partner as a working mother. Also, your colleagues may not view you as a serious professional. No one wants to hear your child coughing in the background during a major conference call." But some firms now offer part-time tracks designed to accommodate the family needs of working mothers while at the same time allowing them to stay on a partnership track. The former accounting attorney voices some skepticism: "Some part-time positions may work. It truly depends on the organization, their management and your direct supervisor. Unfortunately, I know too many part-time working moms who get paid two-thirds of their normal salary, but they still work like they are full-time employees."

Most insiders agree that the working parents who seem to handle best the dual stresses of family life and professional life have help. For many this help comes from a nanny or au pair. Mildeen Worrell, a tax attorney on Capitol Hill, explains how she has successfully juggled her family and career: "I admit being a working mom is difficult. It requires a lot of juggling and you need an understanding and sympathetic boss. You must come to terms that some tradeoffs will be made, like breaking a promise to take your son to see a movie because you have to work late on an emergency project. In my case, I decided that I needed very reliable care for my son so that no matter what happens to my schedule, his schedule stays the same. The use of an au pair makes my life more manageable and keeps my son happy."

Tax Law as a Second Career

Tax law may be a wonderful field for people choosing it as a second career. Those with experience in accounting or business will probably find it easier to switch to a career in tax. According to Lisa Tavares, an employee benefits attorney who worked for an insurance company before going to law school, "Knowing a related field like insurance made it easier for employers to be interested in me for tax-related positions in the employee benefits arena."

For other tax attorneys, their previous careers had nothing to do with taxes. Professor Boise got his start in the criminal justice system: "I came to the law because of an interest in constitutional issues that arose from working as a police officer for several years. Few lawyers find careers in the area of constitutional law, but for me, tax law provided similar satisfactions. First, tax law is based on an extensive, ever-changing statutory regime. Second, particularly as a professor, I have found that tax law provides a laboratory within which to examine the intersection of rules and social policy."

Diversity Issues

As with many niche areas in the law, tax is not a particularly diverse field. "If you look at this as a whole," observes John O'Neill, "there is not enough diversity in tax. This is a problem because there is so much career opportunity, but yet we have a labor shortage. Where will we get the people to fill these vacancies? Diversity can help us do this. After all, tax is colorblind – we all pay taxes." For these reasons, TaxTalent.com started a diversity forum including articles, a discussion board and a mentor program whereby candidates can be matched with diverse mentors in the tax field.

In fact, many organizations, from big law firms and accounting firms to the IRS, have launched programs designed to recruit a more diverse body of tax lawyers. Going to career fairs, recruiting through minority bar associations and forming mentor programs are just some of the efforts these organizations have initiated. Richard Winston, an associate at Steel Hector and Davis LLP, is proud that his firm was voted the "Most Diverse Law Firm in the U.S." for the third year in a row in the spring 2003 issue of the <u>Minority Law Journal</u>. He feels "fortunate to work at a place were diversity is valued." Of the firm's approximately 200 lawyers, 36.9 percent are minorities.

Many bar associations have also increased their efforts on the diversity front. The Tax Section of the American Bar Association has a diversity committee devoted to attracting diverse candidates to the tax profession. Wayne

Hamilton, a former chair of this committee, outlines what he sees as the problem and potential solutions: "We have a pipeline problem. There are simply not enough diverse candidates choosing tax law. So we started a law school program where we set up panel discussions at various law schools with minority tax professionals to show students that this is a real, viable career option. So far we have done these programs at law schools across the country and we hope to make them more annual programs. We also hope to start recruiting people even earlier than law school, like those in undergraduate accounting and business programs and perhaps even some high-schoolers." In addition, says, Hamilton, "We also recently started a mentoring program that will pair interested tax lawyers, typically those who are new to the practice or those who have only been practicing for a few years, with experienced ABA members. So in addition to trying to recruit folks at the law school level we want to give them some guidance and mentorship to help retain them in the profession."

Another reason for limited diversity in the tax profession, according to a tax lawyer in the South, is the field's perceived lack of glamour. "Unless a person has an accounting background, they would probably not think of tax – it's not sexy. They probably think of being a transactional attorney and tax just doesn't come to mind. Also, people don't realize you don't need an accounting background to do this." This attorney adds, "The problem doesn't just end there. We still have stereotyped areas of law for different cultures – African-Americans are labor lawyers or civil rights attorneys, Hispanics are immigration lawyers, and so on. From a hiring perspective, some people still believe in these stereotypes and believe that people of color aren't smart enough to do complex work."

Pro Bono Opportunities

Tax law is an area that lends itself very well to pro bono work. Everyone has to pay taxes, but many low-income taxpayers haven't the means to hire their own tax attorneys and have difficulty understanding and applying complex tax laws. The following paragraphs outline some of the areas in which tax lawyers working pro bono have been able to make an impact.

Tax return preparation (VITA)

The Volunteer Income Tax Assistance Program (VITA) is a program sponsored by the IRS at various locations throughout the country. The IRS trains volunteers to provide free tax preparation assistance to local residents who can't afford to pay for tax help, including the elderly, non-English speaking individuals, those with low or fixed incomes and those with disabilities or special needs. Typically, VITA sites are held at college campuses, local community centers and other easily accessible locations. Because VITA only offers tax return preparation services, the sites, are open from January through April of each year. Hours vary between sites but most are open on weekday nights and on weekends. VITA is an excellent program for tax lawyers who are looking for pro bono activities that only require a few hours a week for a few months. You can find a local VITA site in your area by calling the IRS at 1-800-829-1040 or by reviewing their web site at http://www.irs.treas.gov.

Tax litigation (LITCs)

Low Income Taxpayer Clinics (LITCs) provide legal representation to low-income individuals who have tax disputes with the IRS. These tax disputes are usually over the correct amount owed to the IRS for back taxes. LITCs receive partial funding from the IRS, but the clinics and volunteers are independent of the agency and the federal government. Lawyers who volunteer with these clinics negotiate with the IRS to resolve their clients' tax issues. Sometimes, the issues go to court and volunteers get an opportunity to try cases before the U.S. Tax Court. Law schools, accounting schools and exempt organizations typically run these clinics. They offer wonderful opportunities for those looking for pro bono activities in the controversy area. You can find a local Low Income Taxpayer Clinic in your area by reviewing the list provided on the American Bar Association's web site at http://www.abanet.org/tax/ under the Tax Tips 4 U section. You might also try your local law school, bar association or the IRS.

Exempt organizations

Many small charitable organizations need help organizing their charters, getting tax-exempt status and handling day-to-day tax questions. In most major cities, there is an alliance dedicated to providing pro bono assistance to these organizations. A great way to learn about exempt organizations, while at the same time giving back to your community, is to volunteer with one of these alliances or nonprofits. For example, the Washington Council of Agencies serves as a network for Washington, D.C., metropolitan-based nonprofit groups. The council has nearly 1,000 local nonprofits as members, many of whom are in need of pro bono tax services. Often, local nonprofit organizations contact law firms and accounting firms directly when seeking pro bono advice. Finding a nonprofit to help is fairly easy, and in fact, if you mention your desire at the next firm cocktail party you may be inundated with requests for help.

Wondering what it's like to work at a specific employer?

Read what EMPLOYEES have to say about:
- Workplace culture
- Compensation
- Hours
- Diversity
- Hiring process

Read employer surveys on THOUSANDS of top employers.

VAULT
> the most trusted name in career information™

Go to www.vault.com

A Day in the Life

CHAPTER 7

Tax Associate, Employee Benefits at a Large East Coast Law Firm

8:15 a.m. Arrive at work. Check e-mail and voice mail.

8:30 a.m. Draft 401(k) profit-sharing plan document for client to comply with changes in federal tax law, including drafting required notice to employees.

11:30 a.m. Call a client to discuss an employment agreement. Draft employment agreement regarding the health benefits provided to an employee.

12:30 p.m. Break for lunch.

1:00 p.m. Continue drafting 401(k) plan document.

2:30 p.m. Draft letters to IRS and client regarding submission of the 401(k) plan to the IRS for review and begin drafting IRS application form that is filed to obtain the approval of the plan document language.

3:30 p.m. Contact T. Rowe Price to obtain necessary information regarding number of employees and amount contributed to 401(k) plan that is necessary for the IRS submission.

4:00 p.m. Respond to e-mail from client regarding whether an employee that already took a loan from an employee benefit plan is eligible to take another loan to put a down payment on a home.

4:30 p.m. At the request of a partner, do research regarding whether a plan may sue a participant that was mistakenly overpaid by the plan upon retirement.

6:00 p.m. Continue drafting and revising 401(k) plan document.

7:30 p.m. Go home.

Tax Associate, Corporate/Transactional Tax at a Large Southern Law Firm

8:45 a.m. Arrive at work. Grab Diet Coke (it's free here). Check e-mails and voice mail. Read the headlines e-mail from BNA and Tax Analysts – ask my secretary to print out article that looks interesting.

9:00 a.m. Working on a major stock acquisition – we represent the buyer. Research Sections 338(h)(10) and 338(g) of the Code for possible issues. Also research if there is a controlled foreign corporation issue. Draft an e-mail to client discussing factual and future legal issues to address in completing the transaction.

11:30 a.m. Call senior corporate partner to discuss the tax issues driving this deal.

12:00 p.m. Grab lunch and bring it back to my desk.

12:30 p.m. Switch to another client and draft final revisions to a memorandum in support of the legal position that will be sent to the IRS (National Office) in support of my client's position. This memo will be sent to the IRS in advance of a sit-down conference with them on this issue.

3:30 p.m. Go to a meeting at an accounting firm to discuss a matter that we are working jointly on. Have a telephone conference with a third outside attorney also representing the same client.

5:30 p.m. The second half of my day is just starting. Conference with a tax partner regarding the status on several ongoing client matters. Stop at the vending machine for a candy bar.

5:45 p.m. Come back to the deal that I worked on in the morning and research various tax structuring issues. The goal is to make sure that my client has the best acquisition vehicle – C corporation, an LLC or an S corporation. Also looking at the tax ramifications involved in financing – whether it should be an equity financing or the client should borrow money. Finally, because there are foreign entities involved, I have to look at foreign tax consequences, such as foreign tax credit issues, controlled foreign corporation issues, local tax issues in various countries (e.g., what is the impact under, say, Belgian tax law) and miscellaneous acquisition issues under Section 338(g) of the Code.

8:00 p.m. Wrap-up time. Finish research, look at e-mails to make sure nothing fell through the cracks, do my timesheets.

8:30 p.m. Go home.

Note: Although my practice is corporate tax with international issues, I still have to do other things like exempt organizations. Also, I fielded five to seven 10-minute phone calls throughout the day answering tax questions while I was doing research.

Tax Associate, Corporate Tax at a Large New York Law Firm

7:30 a.m. Check e-mails and voice mails.

9:30 a.m. Arrive at work. I'm one of the first people in the office. Read *Tax Notes Today* and *BNA Daily Tax Report.*

10:00 a.m. Respond to e-mails and voice mails related to several deals that I'm working on.

11:00 a.m. Review and mark up an acquisition agreement. Telephone conference with the client.

12:30 p.m. Call counsel in another country because this is a global acquisition to discuss interplay between U.S. tax rules and non-U.S. tax rules. Looking at successor liability and transfer tax issues that may apply to this deal.

2:00 p.m. Review tax covenants in the agreement covering how tax returns will be filed after the deal and who will bear taxes in what jurisdictions after the deal closes.

3:00 p.m. Get lunch at firm cafeteria and bring back to my desk. Eat at my desk. Respond to e-mail and voice mails.

4:00 p.m. Start working on another deal. We represent the buyer. Have a conference call with seller's counsel regarding comments that I sent to him yesterday on the acquisition agreement.

6:00 p.m. Seller's counsel sends me a revised agreement with his proposals. I review them with a senior tax partner at my firm and then e-mail the proposed agreement to the client.

6:30 p.m. Turn back to the deal from this morning. Complete the markup and e-mail to the client.

10:30 p.m. Review the offering memorandum for a debt offering. Provide comments to corporate lawyer in my firm. Basically, I'm explaining to someone who will buy the bonds what the tax consequences are – it's called the tax disclosure language.

10:45 p.m. Do my timesheets and leave for my secretary to input tomorrow. Finally go home.

Tax Partner, Corporate Tax at a Large West Coast Law Firm

8:00 a.m. Attend committee meeting.

9:00 a.m. Check and respond to e-mail and voice mail. Update and organize "to do" list for the day.

10:00 a.m. Conference call regarding structure for proposed merger.

11:30 a.m. Review and circulate comments regarding draft merger agreement.

12:30 p.m. Break for lunch.

1:15 p.m. Check and respond to e-mail and voice mail.

1:45 p.m. Review and comment on offering circular for [SEC Rule] 144A debt offering; internal conference call regarding same.

3:30 p.m. Conference call with client's accountant regarding impact of financing on net operating losses. Discussion with client regarding same and regarding features of preferred stock offering.

4:15 p.m. Check and respond to e-mail and voice mail.

4:45 p.m. Draft response to IRS request for additional information regarding private letter ruling.

6:00 p.m. Review summer associate memo regarding proposed corporate restructuring.

6:45 p.m. Update timesheets and check and respond to e-mail and voice mail before going home.

9:00 p.m. At home, continue revisions to tax article in preparation for publication.

Solo Practitioner, General Tax Practice on the East Coast

7:30 a.m. Read *The Wall Street Journal* and tax law periodicals.

8:30 a.m. Check e-mails and review case status of active files.

9:00 a.m. Meet with client to discuss estate plan.

9:45 a.m. Meet with client to discuss collection due process hearing with the IRS.

10:15 a.m. Review notes from client meetings and prepare tax strategy for estate plan and collection due process hearing.

11:00 a.m. Meet with IRS revenue agent concerning tax lien placed on client's property and settlement matter.

11:30 a.m. Prepare for appeals conference with IRS.

12:00 p.m. Attend lunch and board of directors meeting of community foundation.

1:30 p.m. Return calls and e-mails. Review mail concerning clients and follow-up, if needed.

2:00 p.m. Meet with client concerning denial of earned income tax credit.

2:30 p.m. Research tax strategies for an estate plan and prepare first draft for client.

3:30 p.m. Gather documents needed for collection due process hearing and review procedural requirements for hearing.

4:00 p.m. Meet with client concerning dischargeability of taxes in bankruptcy.

4:30 p.m. Work on finalizing offer in compromise for client with their CPA.

5:00 p.m. Research tax law issues on estate plan, offer in compromise in preparation to represent my client.

6:00 p.m. Calculate billable hours for the day. Leave at 6:15.

Note: Two unique features of operating a solo practice in a small town are: (1) you are expected to represent the indigent – i.e., cases concerning denial of earned income tax credits; and (2) you are expected to be included in at least one community organization, preferable as a member of the board of directors or as counsel to the organization.

Tax Planning and Controversy Attorney (In-House), Privately-Held Large Corporation

8:00 a.m. Arrive at work. Check voice messages and e-mail. Also check *Tax Notes Today*.

9:00 a.m. Review status of IRS audit.

9:45 a.m. Provide update to vice president of tax and vice president of subsidiary being audited.

10:30 a.m. Meet with tax staff to discuss open items owed to the IRS. Schedule meetings with internal and external employees to get additional information to respond to IRS audit requests.

12:00 p.m. Break for lunch. Have a networking lunch with staff from the subsidiary to see what transactions they are working on and provide them with feedback on how their business practice may be impacted by a proposed IRS position.

1:00 p.m. Review draft responses to IRS document requests.

3:00 p.m. Call and do a status update with the IRS team coordinator assigned to audit the subsidiary. Work with him on scheduling meetings with appropriate staff members of the subsidiary.

4:00 p.m. Work on planning issue. Review outside counsel's opinion on a proposed transaction. Contact outside counsel for clarifications and changes. Contact department that initiated the transaction to explain my concerns.

6:30 p.m. Go home.

Tax Planning Attorney (In-House) Focusing on State and Local Tax, Fortune 500 Corporation in the Midwest

8:30 a.m. Arrive at work. Check e-mail and voice mail. Open up the company internal web site to check out new company news including information on our state and local lobbying efforts.

9:00 a.m. Meet with human resources to discuss amending our adoption assistance program for employees so they may take full advantage of all the tax benefits awarded by the Code due to certain changes in the tax law in 2002 that increased certain exclusions.

10:00 a.m. Conference call with plant manager in one of our corporate sites to discuss a strategy to finance a new entrance to the plant and road improvements through tax increment financing.

11:00 a.m. Talk with assistant regarding the scheduling of upcoming meetings and updating my calendar.

11:30 a.m. Return phone calls and e-mails.

12:00 p.m. Break for lunch. Go to company-subsidized corporate cafeteria. Bring lunch to office and read *The Wall Street Journal* and other periodicals.

1:00 p.m. Meet with state and local tax compliance staff (mostly accountants) to discuss upcoming state audits.

2:00 p.m. Research issue for the accounting department on capitalizing versus expensing certain costs of a special project.

3:30 p.m. Meet with Latin American affiliate's business development partners to discuss third-party deals which may have domestic tax impact.

4:30 p.m. Return phone calls and e-mails.

6:00 p.m. Go home.

Tax Controversy Attorney (In-House), Fortune 500 Corporation in the South

7:30 a.m. Arrive at office (only a few early risers are in). Check and respond to e-mail and voice mail. Read *Tax Notes Today* and *BNA Daily Tax Report* for developments in the law. Read any online news about my company. Skim *The Wall Street Journal* and the local newspaper.

8:30 a.m. Make phone calls to company employees to gather facts needed for a brief that I had started last week but had to put on the back burner to turn my attention to another matter. Get bounced around from employee to employee (nobody seems to know anything); finally get hold of a few people with relevant information; flesh out the facts; draft affidavits based on conversation. Leave messages for other employees who might have relevant info (some will return my call today, some won't).

10:30 a.m. Have a snack, then get cracking on the brief.

11:15 a.m. Receive phone call from a client I represent pro bono in a tax dispute before IRS Appeals (I had left four messages over the past week; just now returning my phone calls). Speak with him about info he needs to get for the appeals officer. He promises he'll get it; I know I'll have this discussion with him another three times before that happens.

11:30 a.m. Break for lunch with some colleagues at a Cajun restaurant within walking distance. Enjoy the camaraderie; get some good tips for handling my pro bono case; sweat from the Cajun spices and hot sauce.

12:30 p.m. Pop into colleagues' offices and find out the status of cases and issues that they're working on. Share what I've been doing and where things stand with my matters. Receive good ideas about other ways to approach various aspects of my cases.

1:30 p.m. Check and respond to e-mail and voice mail. Get back to the brief writing.

2:30 p.m. Team leader on another matter drops into my office (some cases I handle alone, some I'm part of an in-house team, and some I work with outside counsel); she pulls me into a strategy session that consumes most of the afternoon.

4:30 p.m. Grab a snack and return to my office. Return phone call from outside counsel that I'm working with on another matter. Discuss case strategy and divide responsibility for various tasks.

5:00 p.m. Return to drafting the brief. Realize there are points that still need to be researched. Do legal research on Lexis; print out lots of cases.

7:00 p.m. There's nothing that can't wait until tomorrow and almost everyone else has left the office for the day, so I put the cases in my briefcase with the good intention of reading them after I go to the gym and work out.

Tax Partner Focusing on Financial Institutions and Products, Big Four Accounting Firm

8:00 a.m. Arrive at work. Read *Tax Notes Today* and *BNA Daily Tax Report*.

8:30 a.m. Checking e-mails and voice mails.

9:00 a.m. Discussion in my office with mergers and acquisitions tax partner regarding a financing issue concerning a merger transaction that the firm is working on. We represent the buyer.

10:00 a.m. Meeting in my office with counsel on a cross-border financing transaction that I am working on. At approximately noon, we (counsel and I) went to lunch at a local restaurant along with several other tax partners from my accounting firm.

1:00 p.m. Teleconference discussion with a client going over a short-form tax opinion and representation letter that the client is going to sign in connection with an internal corporate restructuring transaction that they plan on executing later that day. We have been working on the opinion for approximately four months.

2:00 p.m. Teleconference discussion with a tax partner and manager in a field office regarding the tax issues arising in connection with a certain cross-border financing transaction that a local client of theirs is considering.

3:00 p.m. Teleconference discussion with several tax partners from both the United States and a foreign country regarding our resolution of certain tax issues regarding a certain cross-border financing transaction. The firm has a number of clients that are interested in implementing the structure.

4:00 p.m. Returning phone calls and responding to electronic mail messages.

5:00 p.m. Editing a draft of a technical memorandum that supports an opinion of the firm issued to a client in connection with a merger transaction. I am focusing on tax issues surrounding the financing for the merger.

6:30 p.m. Complete electronic record of my timesheet reflecting today's time and send electronically.

7:00 p.m. Go home.

Tax Manager Focusing on Estate Planning, Big Four Accounting Firm

9:30 a.m. Arrive at work. Check e-mails and voice mail. Make and return phone calls.

10:00 a.m. Read *Tax Notes Today* and *BNA Daily Tax Report*. Note any significant developments affecting individuals and trusts.

11:00 a.m. Conference call with client's broker regarding transfer of client's stock into irrevocable trust. E-mail to client's attorney regarding status of trust document. Run software projections to show estate tax savings of transferring stock into trust.

12:30 p.m. Grab lunch at nearby deli.

1:00 p.m. Conference call with co-workers regarding Jobs and Growth Tax Relief Reconciliation Act of 2003 (JAGTRRA) and its planning implications for individuals and trusts.

2:30 p.m. Review e-mail from client's attorney regarding trust document. Review trust document to make sure it includes appropriate provisions for federal tax purposes. Conference call with client's attorney regarding same.

3:30 p.m. Prepare article to be distributed firm-wide on a new Tax Court case regarding family limited partnerships.

5:30 p.m. Read and respond to new e-mail. Make and return phone calls.

6:30 p.m. Leave for the day.

IRS Tax Attorney Practicing in Partnership Tax

8:00 a.m. Arrive at work. Check *Tax Notes Today*. Look for any IRS notices, releases and/or cases regarding partnerships. Check *The New York Times* and other periodicals to be up on current news.

8:30 a.m. Review temporary and proposed regulations governing partnership distributions to increase technical proficiency on them, including working on the examples/problems in the regulations.

10:30 a.m. Return phone calls and answer e-mail questions from revenue agents and other IRS lawyers.

12:00 p.m. Break for lunch.

1:00 p.m. Review partnership issue that had been raised by the revenue agent who is auditing a taxpayer. I serve as the field agent's lawyer with respect to these technical partnership issues. Contact the agent to answer my initial questions on the issue. This review includes doing a detailed file and doing additional legal research. Note: This is a complex project that I'm just beginning and I will work on it for several hours each day over the next week.

3:30 p.m. Do my timesheets and weekly report that covers the significant tax work that I did within the last week. Submit both reports to my boss.

4:00 p.m. Logged in two new cases on requests for my legal assistance from other IRS attorneys. Will begin working on these cases over the next few days.

4:30 p.m. Review e-mail on quick partnership question from a revenue agent (should take less than two hours). Begin legal research on the issue. Will finish research on this and reply to the agent tomorrow afternoon.

5:30 p.m. Go home.

Tax Counsel to the House Committee on Ways and Means

Wondering what it's like to work as a tax counsel to a Congressional committee? Here, an attorney working on Capitol Hill gives Vault the inside scoop.

I wish I could describe a typical day on Capitol Hill, but it is impossible to fit a day within a neat time format. When Congress is in session the nature of each day is unique and sometimes unpredictable. The pace and nature of the day depend on whether major legislation (or a legislative issue) for which I am responsible is being considered either by the committee or the full membership of Congress.

Committee level

The committee has a full staff for the Republican members who serve on the committee as well as a staff for the Democratic members. There is a total of 24 Republican members (including the chairman) and 17 Democrats who serve on the committee. The committee has jurisdiction over legislation in the areas of tax, health, trade, Social Security and human resources (welfare reform, food stamps, unemployment and so on). I serve as a tax attorney for the Democratic staff of the committee.

If the committee is about to bring up a bill for consideration (or a major legislative issue for a hearing), a typical day can begin as early as 8:00 or 8:30 a.m. To prepare for this process, the first step is to have a meeting with my chief of staff to discuss the upcoming legislation (or issue); formulate our preparation model; identify policy and political concerns with the legislation (or issue); develop a schedule for briefing legislative assistants (LAs who work for the Democratic members); schedule a caucus for the Democratic members to meet, discuss the legislation and develop their position regarding the legislation (or issue); coordinate with staff of other committees with interest and/or jurisdiction over the legislation (or issue).

Preparing for the LA briefing requires me to prepare a detailed background memorandum (briefing memo) which is distributed to each Democratic member's office. The memo generally provides background information on the legislation, including why the legislation is being considered. It also identifies the issues arising under the legislation, the pros and cons of each of these issues, the position taken on these issues by parties that will be affected by the legislation (including representatives from the private sector, the public sector, employees representatives and government agencies).

This process generally involves a lot of research and meeting with various groups. Sometimes these meetings occur prior to this stage (some groups will begin to request meetings as soon as an issue comes to the surface and before legislative action begins), and often the meetings occur in the middle of all the other chaos surrounding the legislative process. Scheduling meetings and trying to be responsive to groups to hear their views and concerns during this period present a challenge, but remain very critical to maintaining balance within the process. Thus, my time management skills are constantly challenged during this time. The briefing memo is generally compiled during the day (and often late in the evening after regular business hours) with some parts being completed between meeting with various groups, answering calls from members' offices about the pending legislation or some other legislative issue, meeting with staff of other committees and/or government agencies (including Treasury, IRS, Department of Labor and Pension Benefit Guaranty Corporation (PBGC)).

Then comes the actual briefing for the LAs. The briefing will begin with me going over the legislation (or issue for the hearing) highlighting all the relevant issues. The LAs are engaged with questions and/or any additional issues or concerns that could affect their members' constituents. Some of these issues are added to the package for consideration by the members during the member caucus.

If the committee action is a hearing on a major legislative issue (or a specific legislative proposal) all the above steps are duplicated. In addition, the evening before the hearing, I review the testimony of all the witnesses invited to testify and prepare questions of important aspects of their testimony. Also, I identify issues that may be important to a particular member, and have the witnesses address such issues in more detail for the benefit of the member.

The next stage of the process occurs at the member level. At this point all the members are fully aware of the legislation and the relevant issues. A caucus for the Democratic members is scheduled during which the members will discuss Democratic strategy for purposes of committee consideration of the legislation (or hearing). The discussion generally will include whether (in the context of a markup) a Democratic substitute would be offered, what provisions would be included in such substitute and whether the Democrats will offer amendments to the underlying legislation. At that point I would develop amendments. I would work with the House Legislative Counsel's office to have them reduce the goal of each amendment to statutory language, and I would write a corresponding plain English description for each amendment. These would be offered by specific members during the committee's consideration of the legislation. The markup begins with a walk-through of the legislation being considered. Often, I would prepare questions to be asked during this process to highlight issues of concerns the members have with the legislation.

All policy and technical questions a member may have are addressed during this time (or later as additional issues come up).

If the members decide to offer a Democratic substitute, I must work closely with Legislative Counsel to ensure that the goals are translated to statutory language. I then prepare a plain English explanation to accompany the legislative language. In addition, a summary description of the substitute is prepared for each member and for distribution to individuals attending the markup.

For actual consideration of the legislation in the committee, preparation is required the day before (often working very late into the night). The package generally includes a summary of the legislation being put forth; amendments to the legislation (both in legislative language and description of each); questions regarding important issues; legislative package for any Democratic substitute being offered; summary of the Democratic substitute; comparison sheet of the advantages and disadvantages of the two legislative packages (chairman's mark and Democratic substitute); talking points in support of the amendments and/or Democratic substitute; talking points on issues of interest to the members from the underlying legislation.

During both a markup of legislation and a hearing, I must be available to all the Democratic members to respond to any questions that come up or to explain particular issues that may require technical input.

After the bill is reported out by the committee, I must prepare views of the Democratic members which may be additional views (if there is general agreement with the underlying legislation) but the Democrats have strong feelings about other issues that were not addressed, or dissenting views (if there is generally disagreement with the underlying legislation). The views must be written and circulated to our members to be signed generally within one or two legislative days. This deadline is important because the Democratic (minority) views must be ready when the legislation is filed with the House to be placed on the calendar for consideration by the full House.

Full Congress level

A process very similar to the one described above applies when legislation is being brought to the House floor for consideration by the House of Representatives. The element that changes most is that I work with a wider membership. All the members of the House must familiarize themselves with the upcoming legislation to decide how they will vote. Helping the members and their staff understand the legislation is a critical aspect of this process.

In addition to the stages outlined at committee level, statements for the Rules Committee must be prepared, as well as multiple copies of any Democratic substitute. It is very possible that the substitute offered on the floor will be somewhat different from the one offered in committee. This is necessary to accommodate the broader memberships (and correspondingly diverse issues) as well as interest of other committees of jurisdiction. These changes must be reflected in the statutory language and the description/summary of the legislation.

Materials on the legislation must be prepared and made available for House-wide caucus and floor consideration at least the day before the legislation is brought to the floor. The timing under which legislation is brought to the floor is decided by the majority party (in this case the Republicans), so it is totally out of our control. It can happen at any time including very early in the morning or very late at night. I must be present on the floor during consideration of the legislation to respond to any questions members or their staff may have about the legislation or to handle unforeseen emergencies.

Before the legislation is brought to the floor, I must work closely with the parliamentarian to ensure that all the provisions included in the Democratic substitute are drafted in a manner that would not violate the House rules (for example, all the provisions are germane to the underlying legislation; does not violate any Budget Points of Order). In some cases, this step may be necessary for committee consideration but slightly different rules apply for committee markup and Floor consideration.

Preparing for conference

All tax legislation must originate in the House; thus, after the House has completed action on tax legislation, the Senate will pass similar legislation. The timing for the Senate to take action on a tax bill that has been passed by the House is independently determined by the Senate.

Generally, after the House has passed the legislation, and before it is taken up by the Senate, I will have discussions with the Democratic staff of the corresponding committee, the Senate Finance Committee (and sometimes the Committee on Health, Education, Labor and Pensions) regarding the Democratic strategy and policy goals of the legislation.

After the Senate has passed similar tax legislation, the two bills must be reconciled. The goal generally is to resolve the differences between the two bills with each chamber (House and Senate) receiving most of their legislative provisions in the final bill. Very often, this must be accomplished within budget and revenue constraints. The conference generally is conducted by a few members from the House and the Senate who serve on committees of jurisdiction.

The provisions that are the same in both bills usually survive but is it not unheard of to have provisions that are the same in both bills be modified in conference. The more difficult part of this process is dealing with provisions that are different in both bills, or are not included in either version of the legislation. This is a process of intense negotiations both at the members and staff level. Staff from both chambers must ensure that every agreed upon item is correctly drafted and described for the final conference agreement. Upon completion of the conference, a single bill that represents both the House and the Senate is brought back to the House and the Senate to be voted on by the full membership of each chamber (see steps involved when legislation is brought to the House floor).

Summary

My duties in the capacity of tax attorney for the committee involve many more duties but the most significant aspects have been described above.

GETTING HIRED

Chapter 8: Education

Chapter 9: Hiring Process

Chapter 10: The Interview

Education

CHAPTER 8

There is no single, surefire way to get hired as a tax attorney. Some tax lawyers get their first jobs through on-campus recruiting at their law schools, while others attend job fairs or send cover letters and resumes to prospective employers.

The next three chapters outline the three main components in establishing a career in tax law:

- Education: how much and what kind you will need

- The hiring process: from job fairs and on-campus interviews to networking through professional organizations and mentors

- Cover letters, resumes and addenda: tips on drafting effective cover letters and resumes, along with critiqued samples

Different Educational Paths

A legal education is a prerequisite to becoming a tax lawyer. But what else do you need? An accounting background? An advanced degree in taxation? The answer often depends on whom you ask. In fact, if you ask nine average tax lawyers how they found their niche, you'll likely get nine different answers. Witness the range of responses from these practitioners:

• *I knew I wanted to be an accountant back in high school, so from that point on everything I did educationally revolved around increasing my background. I majored in accounting in college and developed an interest in tax from these classes.* – Richard Larkins, a tax partner with Ernst & Young LLP in Washington, D.C.

• *I spent my whole life actually running from tax. After an undergraduate degree in psychology and marketing and two graduate degrees, including a JD and an MBA in marketing, it wasn't until I started my LL.M in securities regulation that I decided to give tax a try. It wasn't until I added it as a major that I realized I was interested in tax.* – Allen Madison, a tax associate at Fenwick & West LLP in Silicon Valley.

• *I chose tax because it's one of the only subjects where you take a course in law school and it translates into real life – civil procedure has little relevance in actual practice. Section 61 of the Code, which you will learn in your first* tax class, follows you for the rest of your life. – Richard Winston, a tax associate with Steel, Hector & Davis LLP in Miami.

Law school is where I got the 'bug' for tax. I took my first federal income tax class and liked the policy and legislative issues, especially given my undergraduate background in political science. – Melinda Merk, a tax manager with a Big Four accounting firm in Washington, D.C.

Tax was completely an accident! I used to say that I would never do tax because it changes all the time. It wasn't until I took a job with the Internal Revenue Service and got an LL.M in tax that I gave into my true tax interest. – Lisa Tavares, a tax associate with a Washington, D.C., law firm.

I went to law school to practice constitutional law. I had no interest in tax. In fact, my wife persuaded me to take basic federal income tax so that we could prepare our own tax returns. To her surprise, and mine, I actually liked the class and began to 'load up' on other tax classes. – Craig Boise, a tax professor at Case Law School in Cleveland, Ohio.

Although I got my BS in accounting, I never really considered tax as a career option. It wasn't until I joined my first law firm as a corporate associate that I noticed the true high flyers were those who were the stars in niche areas. Because of my accounting background, I believed tax was a natural niche area for me. I decided to make the switch from a general corporate practice to tax. – Randle Pollard, a tax attorney with a large corporation in Indianapolis, Ind.

When I started law school, I was interested in corporate law until a career counselor steered me toward tax. The reason he gave, which struck a chord with me, was that many associates in corporate law practices wind up doing mind-numbing work while tax associates almost always get intellectually challenging assignments from day one. My observation since I've been in practice – speaking with friends and colleagues in both tax and corporate practices – is that my career counselor was correct. – Pete Lowy, a tax attorney with a major corporation.

I had no real interest in tax. I kind of fell into tax by just being a good student. I did very well in my tax class and my tax professor encouraged me to apply for an internship with the Internal Revenue Service because he knew the head of hiring in the local field office. After that internship, I knew that I wanted to pursue a career in tax. – Shelia Dansby Harvey, a tax attorney with the Internal Revenue Service in Houston, Texas.

Although all may not have traveled the same route, many lawyers agree that the following kinds of background can help prepare you for a tax career:

- Accounting background or master's degree in taxation
- Tax classes in law school
- LL.M in taxation
- Continuing education courses

Accounting Background

Although an accounting degree is not necessary, tax attorneys must be familiar with accounting practices. Some lawyers have formal accounting training either because they majored in accounting as undergraduates or because they are enrolled agents or certified public accountants. Others may not have had formal training in accounting but have managed to learn on the job.

According to TaxTalent.com's John O'Neill, "An accounting background is not required. In fact, many tax lawyers have no formal accounting training. But if you don't have this training coming out of school it is highly advisable that you be prepared to take some classes. Understanding accounting concepts is crucial in the tax profession because you must be able to look at a financial statement and understand tax accounting versus GAAP (generally accepted accounting principles)."

Tax attorney Wayne Hamilton found formal accounting classes helpful. He explains, "I decided to take a few accounting classes at night while I was already practicing. They have been invaluable to helping me understand the business side of my job and also in my interactions with the accounting group and their concern about the financial statement impact of a particular issue." The accounting classes that might be most helpful as a foundation for tax lawyers include:

- Introduction to accounting
- Financial accounting
- Intermediate accounting

These classes are offered at most four-year universities and at many local community colleges.

Some law schools now offer an accounting class for lawyers. For example, at the University of Virginia School of Law, students can enroll in "Accounting: Understanding and Analyzing Financial Statements." The course reviews accounting terminology, generally accepted accounting standards, and the differences between financial accounting (i.e., accounting for financial statements) and income tax accounting (i.e., accounting for income tax returns).

Other tax attorneys receive no formal training. Peter Lowy, a tax lawyer in Houston, says, "Most of the accounting I know I learned on the job." To supplement this on-the-job training, many lawyers take continuing legal or professional education classes (known as CLEs or CPEs), which are typically one- or two-day courses focused on a particular subject. For example, Practicing Law Institute, or PLI, offers many classes that explain basic accounting and finance concepts, like "Accounting & Finance: What Every Practicing Lawyer Needs to Know." Many courses are also offered by local bar associations and CPA societies. The California CPA Education Foundation offers several basic courses, including "Financial Statement Disclosures for the Tax Practitioner" and "Accounting and Auditing for the Tax Practitioner."

Master's Degree in Taxation

In addition to having an accounting background, some tax attorneys choose to enhance their education by getting a master's degree in taxation, known as an MST. The typical MST program takes one year (three to five years if attending part time) and usually requires 24 credit units or 10 to 12 classes. Some schools offer executive programs. For example, at the University of Virginia McIntire School of Commerce, a working professional can obtain a master's degree in accounting/tax consulting in one year by attending two weeklong sessions and weekend classes over 17 weekends.

Although the classes offered in an MST program vary depending on the school, many programs suggest that the following subjects be taken as core classes:

- Federal individual tax
- International tax
- Corporate tax
- Tax research and writing
- Tax policy
- Taxation of flow-through entities (partnerships, limited liability companies, S corporations)

These master's programs also offer numerous electives and provide students with the opportunity to focus on a particular tax specialty. For example, a student interested in corporate tax law may take electives like mergers and acquisitions, taxation of business operations or corporate consolidations.

In order to earn an MST, most programs require that you have taken certain prerequisites as an undergraduate, including one or two introductory accounting classes, an intermediate accounting class and two federal taxation classes. Those political science majors who never took an accounting class in college needn't worry, however; it's not too late to bone up. Most of these prerequisites can be taken at a local community college.

Some law schools even have joint programs with accounting schools that allow students to earn an MST while in law school. For example, at the University of Southern California Leventhal School of Accounting, a student can get a master's in business taxation while working toward a law degree.

Tax Classes in Law School

Because tax laws often impact other areas of the law, many law schools encourage every student to take at least one tax course, usually a basic federal tax class. Affectionately known as "baby tax" or "easy tax" by practicing tax lawyers, the course typically covers federal income tax issues for individuals. According to Randle Pollard, a former tax professor, "The basic federal income tax class covers the fundamentals of income, exemptions and exclusions from tax and deductions. Students will get an overview of our federal tax system, including how it is shaped by the IRS, Treasury and Congress."

In addition to basic federal tax, many law schools offer corporate tax classes. These classes cover tax issues involved in the formation, operation, reorganization and liquidation of corporations. For students interested in practicing transactional corporate law, this class is a must. Even for students interested in other tax specialties, having a basic understanding of the corporate tax laws is very helpful and highly recommended.

Some law schools allow students virtually to major in tax law. These schools offer some five or more tax classes in their normal three-year curriculum ranging from federal income tax (a.k.a. "baby tax") and corporate tax to partnership tax, estate and gift tax, and state and local tax. The University of Florida School of Law offers several tax courses for students enrolled in its JD program. Similarly, the University of Virginia School of Law offers a tax law concentration where students can take some 12 tax law classes in the law school. Schools with strong tax LL.M programs often offer numerous tax law classes to JD candidates. Both Georgetown University Law Center and New

York University School of Law offer more than 40 tax law classes in their regular JD programs, many of which are also part of the LL.M program.

The LL.M Debate

LL.M is Latin for Legum Magister or Master of Laws. It is an academic postgraduate law degree earned after obtaining a JD. LL.Ms are offered in many legal specialties including healthcare law, international law, environmental law, intellectual property law and, of course, tax law.

LL.Ms in tax typically last for one year (three to five years if done part time) and require 24 credit hours or eight to ten tax classes. Schools on the quarter system, like Harvard University, may require more classes. Students in LL.M programs gain in-depth knowledge in various tax specialties and further develop their research and writing skills. Basic LL.M. classes include:

- Research and writing
- Partnerships
- Timing
- Property
- Individual income tax
- Corporate income tax
- Procedure

According to John O'Neill, advantages to earning an LL.M in taxation include a deeper understanding of tax laws, improved research and writing skills, a second advanced degree that should increase your value to future employers and a better chance of placement in the tax profession (particularly if you attend a top LL.M program).

So do you really need an LL.M? Several practitioners weigh in on the debate. One attorney with an LL.M believes that "top-tier law firms still care more about where you got your JD and your class rank." Another tax lawyer explains, "In terms of finding a tax position, the LL.M helps mainly if you went to a lower-tier law school. LL.Ms in such cases push the ball a little further up the hill. If you go to a top-10 law school, an LL.M is probably not that crucial, at least in terms of landing a job. No one's going to say you graduated top of the class at Stanford but we aren't going to hire you and let you do tax because you don't have an LL.M." According to Fenwick & West attorney Allen Madison, "Although an LL.M adds value, if you take enough tax classes in law school and have other credentials like a CPA, master's in taxation or even an MBA, an LL.M may not be necessary."

MST vs. LL.M

In fact, these other degrees may be more helpful to your tax career depending on the nature of your practice. John O'Neill discusses the differences between the Master of Laws and a master's degree in taxation: "MST and LL.M degrees have similarities because they are focused on tax; however, there are nuances that separate the two (in most cases). The coursework for the LL.M in tax generally has a slant toward the legal side of tax and focuses on research, writing and litigation. The coursework for the MST, while covering some of these areas, also brings in the finance, accounting, treasury and business ramifications of tax. Some schools that offer both degree programs share some of the classes between the degrees."

Which degree is better? According to O'Neill, "This depends on your intended use. If you have a JD and are going to do research, planning and writing, then the LL.M makes good sense. If you would rather look at the financial aspects and business side, maybe the MST is for you. As with any advanced degree program, part of the benefit is just the discipline and extra effort it takes to attain the degree."

Peer pressure

Some lawyers argue that the intellectual pursuit of an LL.M cannot be matched. Attorney Randle Pollard says, "Even though I had an accounting background and went to a top-tier law school, I did not take very many tax classes and in fact started out in my law firm as a corporate associate. I felt I needed an LL.M to increase my tax training and to legitimately be considered a tax attorney." An LL.M may put you on equal footing with your peers, as Pollard notes. "I thought the LL.M would speed up my career path," he says, "but it actually put me on par with many of my colleagues. Most of the successful tax professionals that I knew had LL.Ms." Wayne Hamilton, a tax attorney in Florida, agrees: "I think an LL.M is mostly necessary because most of your peers have one." In fact, for some tax positions, like teaching jobs, an LL.M is almost a prerequisite.

A career boost

Finally, an LL.M may be career enhancing even if it is not essential. According to John O'Neill, "An LL.M can be a career boost, particularly if you work for a company or firm that believes the LL.M is important. The amount of the boost is determined by myriad factors like the school you get your JD from and your class rank, the school you get your LL.M from, the type of work you will do, the organization you work for and the tax market in the location in which you live." This boost may translate into a financial gain. Although there's no comprehensive study on the amount of compensation that an LL.M may add to your career, O'Neill notes that "typically an LL.M does make more than a JD when first graduating from school, but the real differences come from applying the knowledge you have gained in the tax profession and leveraging into better and better tax positions throughout your career." O'Neill adds, "An LL.M will not guarantee anything but it may help."

Still, some tax attorneys believe that an LL.M is not necessary if you already have a job at a top tax law firm or accounting firm. Richard Larkins, a partner at Ernst & Young, observes, "LL.Ms are about marketing. If you can already market yourself based on your law school degree, your accounting and tax background and/or your work experience, you probably don't really need it."

Where to go?

Once you've decided to pursue an LL.M, the next important decision is to determine where you will go. According to *U.S. News & World Report*, the top three tax law programs are offered by New York University, University of Florida and Georgetown University. There are also several regional and local programs. TaxTalent.com has a database of graduate tax programs, which you can search by location and type (e.g., part-time, full-time and even online). You can also find a listing of Master of Laws programs worldwide at www.llm-guide.com.

Many attorneys strongly believe that where you get your LL.M matters. Lisa Tavares, an employee benefits attorney with a major law firm, suggests, "Going to a top-tier LL.M program is important, especially for people who didn't do well in law school. It's often a second chance for students to prove themselves while showing their genuine interest in the tax field." But top LL.M programs are often expensive – around $30,000 for tuition alone. Is it really necessary to spend this money when there is a good, local LL.M program at a fraction of the cost? Again, the answer depends on your situation.

Take the fictional student Jimmie A. Taxhopeful. Jimmie attended a second-tier law school in the Midwest where he was in the top third of his class. He took a few accounting classes in college and two tax classes in law school. He is now interested in pursuing a career in tax law. He would like to live in the Midwest and wonders whether he should attend a local school with an

LL.M program or a top-tier LL.M program elsewhere. He is also concerned about the cost of obtaining the degree since he has already amassed debt from his undergraduate studies and law school. What should he do? Different experts weigh in:

John O'Neill of TaxTalent.com reasons, "This is where that 'local school' factor can kick in. If Jimmie wants a job at, say, one of the top-tier law firms in Chicago, he should probably go for the top LL.M school – especially since he has a second-tier JD. If he is fortunate enough to get a job straight out of law school with a law firm or an accounting firm he should seriously consider working and looking into a part-time LL.M program locally. It might do him better financially both short and longterm."

"If I had a job," says Richard Larkins at Ernst & Young, "I wouldn't quit my job to get an LL.M, because the principal benefit of an LL.M is helping you get a job. But supplementing your job by doing a night LL.M program may make sense. However, you will probably learn more tax working than going back to school. If you don't have a job and went to a less well-known law school, then go to the top LL.M program that you can get into."

Randle Pollard, a tax lawyer with a major corporation, leans toward a top-tier program: "If Jimmie is from, say, Chicago and wants to stay in Chicago for the rest of his life, then a local program may make sense. But if he has any thoughts of wanting to leave Chicago for another city, it will be easier to find a position with an LL.M from one of the top three programs."

According to Calvin Allen, a solo practitioner in Key West, Jimmie should be more concerned with the specifics of each school's program: "Jimmie should go to whichever school has the curriculum that matches the area that he wants to specialize in. So if the local program has a great international focus and this is what he wants to do, Jimmie should go to the local school. I would go to a less prestigious school if they had the curriculum that I wanted."

Finally, an East Coast tax attorney votes hands down for prestige: "Jimmie should go to New York University. It's the only way to get into a large law firm. He will likely have problems getting hired even by a regional law firm if he goes to the local school. Even students who go to the top programs have problems getting the big law firm jobs. Unless you are in the top 10 people or so from NYU (or top three to five from Georgetown and Florida), the LL.M is just not the equalizer for a poor law school. However, if he wants a job at an accounting firm or the IRS, the importance of getting an LL.M from a top program may not be as crucial."

Continuing Education

Tax laws are always changing. In 2003 alone there were many tax law changes. In fact, The Jobs and Growth Tax Relief Reconciliation Act signed by President Bush in May 2003 represents the third-largest tax cut in U.S. history. Perhaps there is no other area in the law in which continuing education is more important than tax law. Therefore, in addition to getting a great tax background and gaining an understanding of accounting principles and concepts, tax professionals must stay abreast of new tax laws by taking continuing legal education classes, or CLEs.

Much of this continuing education is offered by bar associations. The American Bar Association's Section of Taxation, with over 20,000 members, is the largest tax-focused professional organization. The ABA Tax Section holds conferences three times a year at various locations across the country, including its May meeting which is always held in Washington, D.C. Randle Pollard, a tax attorney in Indianapolis, touts the benefits of ABA courses: "The CLE courses offered by the ABA Tax Section provide cutting-edge information on the latest tax laws for all tax specialties. They also provide comprehensive seminars on the nuts and bolts of a variety of tax specialties. The information is helpful for the seasoned tax lawyer and the tax law beginner alike."

State bar associations also often have very active tax committees. These committees are particularly helpful in tracking developments in state tax laws. Some states like California and New York as well as the District of Columbia have tax committees that focus on federal tax issues. Professor Boise at Case Law School comments on the benefits of local bar courses: "A great way to network and to get CLE credits, which are required by most state bar associations, is through programs sponsored by local bar associations." Melinda Merk, who works at a Big Four accounting firm, agrees: "CLE courses offered by local bar associations are often very affordable, especially since they don't require you to travel. Also, they are a great way to network with local tax attorneys and to find out what's hot in a particular tax area."

Several other organizations offer continuing education classes. ALI-ABA is one of the premier organizations offering continuing professional education classes for lawyers. Alliance for Tax, Legal and Accounting Seminars (ATLAS) also offers tax law CLEs. Some organizations focus on a particular tax specialty. The Council for International Tax Education, Inc. (CITE), for example, concentrates on international tax courses and seminars. Similarly, the Council On State Taxation (COST) offers courses on state and local tax issues.

On TaxTalent.com, you'll find a searchable database of tax training courses for every level of tax professional – the beginner, the seasoned practitioner and the expert. A recent search for international tax classes in the Washington, D.C., area yielded three upcoming classes including an introduction to international tax, an intermediate course in international tax and an annual class sponsored by George Washington University on emerging issues in international tax.

Finally, law firms, accounting firms, corporations and government agencies often offer their own in-house training. As a summer intern with the IRS, I received a primer on tax law, tax research and the inter-workings of the federal government agencies handling tax matters. This in-house training was invaluable and it would have been difficult to obtain all of this information in a CLE class. The Big Four accounting firms particularly are known for their emphasis on in-house training. Newly hired attorneys attend week-long classes on many substantive tax topics. Similar advanced classes are offered for more senior tax professionals. Law firms also provide in-house training. According to a tax attorney in the Northeast, "My law firm had weekly tax technical lunches that were actually very valuable. These biweekly lunches were led by a different partner each time and were geared for junior associates. At each lunch the partner would focus on various topics such as choice of entity, drafting documents and so on."

Losing sleep over your job search?
Endlessly revising your resume?
Facing a work-related dilemma?

Super-charge your career with Vault's newest career tools: Resume Reviews, Resume Writing and Career Coaching.

Vault Resume Writing

On average, a hiring manager weeds through 120 resumes for a single job opening. Let our experts write your resume from scratch to make sure it stands out.

- Start with an e-mailed history and 1- to 2-hour phone discussion
- Vault experts will create a first draft
- After feedback and discussion, Vault experts will deliver a final draft, ready for submission

Vault Resume Review

- Submit your resume online
- Receive an in-depth e-mailed critique with suggestions on revisions within TWO BUSINESS DAYS

Vault Career Coach

Whether you are facing a major career change or dealing with a workplace dilemma, our experts can help you make the most educated decision via telephone counseling sessions.

- Sessions are 45-minutes over the telephone

"I have rewritten this resume 12 times and in one review you got to the essence of what I wanted to say!"

– S.G. Atlanta, GA

"It was well worth the price! I have been struggling with this for weeks and in 48 hours you had given me the answers! I now know what I need to change."

– T.H. Pasadena, CA

"I found the coaching so helpful I made three appointments!"

– S.B. New York, NY

For more information go to
www.vault.com/careercoach

VAULT
> the most trusted name in career information™

Hiring Process

CHAPTER 9

For most law students, the primary means of getting a job is still through either on-campus recruiting or targeted mailing of resumes. Experienced tax professionals typically use legal recruiters or job boards to secure new positions.

One of the best places to find information about a potential employer is through NALP forms. The National Association of Law Placement (NALP) publishes the NALP Directory of Legal Employers, which contains information on more than 1,500 employers nationwide. NALP forms can be found at most law schools and many organizations include a copy of their form on their own web site. NALP also maintains an electronic version of the forms on its web site at www.nalpdirectory.com. The NALP form provides basic information about the organization such as salary, size and legal practice areas. In trying to locate tax positions, the online version of the NALP forms is invaluable because it allows you to search only for tax positions and can also be limited by the employer's location and size.

The first part of this chapter focuses on five basic avenues that you can use to get hired: on-campus recruiting, legal recruiters, job boards, mass mailings and job fairs. The second part discusses other things that you can do to enhance your marketability, including interview tips, internships, networking, publishing articles and public speaking, and keeping current with tax and business news.

On-Campus Recruiting

By far the most common method for a law student to get a job is via the on-campus recruiting program. Almost all law schools have such programs whereby employers are matched with law students who meet certain criteria that the employer is seeking. Typically, law students submit resumes to employers planning to visit the school. The employers sift through the resumes and select the students whom they are interested in interviewing. The school provides the employer with an interview room and an interview schedule for those chosen few. Each interview is usually 30 minutes long. Many interviewers are alumni of the particular law school. Of the 15 to 20 students interviewed, two or three might be lucky enough to get a callback interview (a second interview at the employer's offices).

Many law firms provide a list of the schools they plan to visit for on-campus recruiting on their web site. The biggest or most prestigious employers may interview at top schools across the country. For example, for Baker Botts LLP, a 650-lawyer firm based in Texas, the 2003 on-campus recruiting schedule listed visits to over 25 law schools across the country. Medium-sized and smaller organizations may only recruit at local or regional law schools.

Headhunters

Legal recruiters are also a good resource for those seeking legal tax positions, although most recruiters handle experienced lawyers rather than recent graduates. These recruiters, also known as headhunters, may concentrate on jobs in a particular city or region. Some legal recruiters focus exclusively on tax positions. For example, TaxSearch, Inc. devotes all of its recruiting efforts to tax positions both in the United States and abroad.

Typically, corporations or firms contact legal recruiters, asking them to identify candidates that meet the qualifications of the position they are seeking to fill. The headhunter then contacts individuals directly and/or posts ads in legal periodicals or on Internet job sites. Once a pool of candidates is located, the recruiter acts as middleman in arranging interviews between candidates and the prospective employer. A good recruiter will also prepare a candidate for an interview by telling him all about the job itself and the people he would be working with and providing an overview of the organization and its working environment.

Legal recruiters usually only get paid through a referral fee paid by the employer if the employer chooses one of their candidates. This fee is often a percentage of the negotiated salary (e.g., 30 percent of the candidate's first year salary). Ordinarily, the candidate does not pay the legal recruiter. When dealing with a recruiter, John O'Neill advises, "You should foster a good relationship with your headhunter. In other words, treat them right, return their calls, do not bug them, give and get referrals. Keep in mind, if done right, this should be a career-long relationship, not just for when you are looking for a job."

Finding a legal recruiter in your area is fairly straightforward. Many advertise in local bar association periodicals or other magazines and papers geared toward attorneys. Also, talk to other practicing attorneys in your area; some will undoubtedly be able to give you the name of a good headhunter.

Job Boards

Online job boards have gained popularity in the past few years. Thanks to companies like Monster.com, finding potential jobs online has become an extremely important option for the job seeker. In addition to general job boards, there are a few places where you can conduct more targeted searches. Vault.com hosts the Vault Law Job Board, with hundreds of full-time positions at all levels. FindLaw (http://careers.findlaw.com) has a job database where you can search for legal positions by location and practice area. This database primarily contains jobs at law firms. TaxTalent.com also sponsors a database of tax positions. This database allows searches by region, tax specialty, title and position. It includes jobs with many different kinds of organizations and lists tax positions for attorneys and accountants alike.

Mass Mailing

In an age of computers, it may be surprising, but the old-fashioned letter and envelope mass-mailing route is still a viable means of finding a job. When doing a mass mailing you should include a cover letter, a resume and an addendum. Many positions also require writing samples and recommendations. For example, the U.S. Department of Justice, Tax Division, Civil Trial Section, asks that applicants include a resume, a cover letter highlighting relevant experience, law school and any advanced degree transcripts, a list of three professional references and a writing sample.

For law firms, a good place to get information to use in your mass mailing efforts is through NALP forms. These forms may be obtained online at www.nalpdirectory.com. They provide detailed information for job seekers, including an overview of the firm's practice specialties, contact information, demographics of lawyers, salary range and benefits, a list of schools where they conduct on-campus interviews and details on how many interns and new lawyers they hire each year.

So does mass mailing really work? For Allen Madison, a Silicon Valley attorney, this approach did not work directly, but his persistence eventually paid off. As Madison explains, "I first applied to Fenwick & West when I was getting my LL.M at Georgetown University Law Center. I sent a blind cover letter and resume but I received a rejection letter. During my clerkship with the Tax Court, I re-applied to Fenwick & West, and again received a rejection letter. Then, as my clerkship was ending, Fenwick & West announced that they were looking for tax litigators and circulated a flier around the Tax Court to recruit. The third time was the charm – I got the job! In fact, I received my offer letter about one month after receiving my second rejection letter."

Lisa Tavares, an employee benefits attorney with a major law firm, believes that mass mailing can work and suggests, "If sending a letter to a law firm, it is probably more effective if sent to an attorney in the practice group that you want to work in – particularly if you have networked with this person through such places as local bar associations." According to another lawyer, "Mass mailing is practically the only way to get a clerkship with a Tax Court judge."

Job Fairs

Job fairs offer another opportunity for prospective tax lawyers. The National Association of Law Placement is a great resource; the NALP web site lists many of the job fairs held around the country (www.nalp.org/schools/fairlist.htm).

Most job fairs have a central theme or focus. Many are based in a particular region. For example, the North Carolina Law School Consortium Small Firm Job Fair is held each March and April in eastern and western North Carolina and draws employers from law firms with fewer than 15 attorneys. Other fairs focus on recruiting minorities. For example, the Sunbelt Minority Conference offers employers across the country the opportunity to interview minority law students from five states: Arizona, Louisiana, New Mexico, Oklahoma and Texas. Similarly, the Cook County Bar Association Minority Student Job Fair held each fall in Chicago is geared toward minority students looking for positions with law firms and other employers in the Midwest. One job fair that has gained a lot of popularity in recent years was launched by a corporation. The Dupont Primary Law Firm Minority Job Fair was started by Fortune 50 company, E.I. Dupont de Nemours & Co., Inc. This job fair is held every fall in four different cities and attempts to match minority law students with law firms who represent Dupont.

Many law schools also offer their students the opportunity to reach geographically distant markets by participating in job fairs known as off-campus recruiting fairs. The law school partners with several other law schools to sponsor a job fair in a major city that is open only to students of the participating law schools. Students are usually responsible for covering the costs of their travel and lodging while at the fair. For example, the University of Wisconsin Law School participates in the Washington, D.C., Off-Campus Recruitment Program along with five other schools. This off-campus recruitment program is designed to expand interview opportunities for students looking for positions with government agencies and law firms in the Washington, D.C., area. Since employers from D.C. aren't likely to do on-campus recruiting at the University of Wisconsin, these off-campus recruiting job fairs allow students a more direct approach to potential employers than they would otherwise have.

There is even a job fair targeted specifically at LL.Ms. The LL.M in Taxation Job Fair is held every February in Washington, D.C., and is sponsored by Georgetown University Law Center, New York University School of Law, University of Florida School of Law and Boston University School of Law. At this job fair, LL.M students from these schools get a chance to meet with prospective employers from law firms, accounting firms and government agencies.

For those interested in teaching tax law, the job fair sponsored by the Association of American Law Schools (AALS) is the most common route for obtaining an academic position. AALS holds a Faculty Recruitment Conference (known as the "meat market") every October in Washington, D.C. Prior to this job fair, interested attorneys submit an online form and a fee to AALS and their information is included in a distribution booklet sent to law schools. The law schools then pre-select those whom they want to interview. The selected candidates are interviewed over a three-day period in the fall. Some are later invited back for a more in-depth interview at the specific law school.

Increasing Your Marketability

In getting a good job, Ernst & Young partner Richard Larkins says that "the most critical thing you can do is still to go to the best law school that you can get into. But once that is done there are still other things that can help increase your marketability." From internships to developing a relationship with a tax professor at your law school, these extra efforts can help show your commitment to tax. This commitment may be necessary, especially if you didn't go to a top-tier law school or you didn't decide that tax was for you until your last year of school. "The bottom line," according to TaxTalent.com's John O'Neill, "is that you need to show your commitment to tax. If things in your background are lacking, work on them. Buy better clothes/shoes, take a public speaking course, read journals. If this means not getting the big law firm job right away, don't despair. Instead, try for a position that will give you good tax training like with the IRS. Become a doer instead of a watcher."

Internships

Perhaps the best way to increase your marketability is through the hands-on training of an internship. Most organizations have internship programs of some sort. On-campus recruiting, job fairs, job boards and mass mailing with NALP forms are all excellent ways to locate and apply for internships. Although many internships are for summer positions, there are also opportunities for internships during the year while you are in school. Some internships may be unpaid, but the experiences you gain can be invaluable and help you decide which area of tax you are most interested in. They can also go a long way in setting your resume apart from the next candidate.

Shelia Dansby Harvey, a tax attorney with the Internal Revenue Service, encourages students to seek out school-year internships: "Summer internships are great, but they are certainly very competitive. Internships during the school year give students an opportunity to be exposed to just as many opportunities – perhaps even more – and for some reason fewer people apply for them. Many of the school-year internships are unpaid, but some schools do offer class credit."

Publishing articles and public speaking

One way to show your interest in tax while increasing your marketability is through publishing articles. Publishing helped Calvin Allen, a solo practitioner in Florida, land a dream job with the government. "I had the opportunity of a lifetime working with the Treasury Department's Office of International Affairs," he says. "They started a tax program where they send tax advisors to different countries to help develop tax laws. I applied for the job along with many other candidates and was selected to go to South Africa. I spent three weeks in South Africa working with the director of tax policy in the minister of finance's office for South Africa. I got to help develop tax laws and recommend changes to existing laws. For example, I got to help shape tax issues related to charitable contributions, such as what constitutes a contribution and how you value it. I was told that a key decision in picking me for the job was all of the articles and comments that I wrote on international issues (particularly those that impact South Africa)."

Publishing is particularly helpful for those interested in teaching. Professor Boise of Case Law School explains, "As a professor, you are expected to publish articles. The old saying, 'Publish or perish,' is accurate in this regard. Having previous experience in writing law review-length articles can help you in landing a job in academia." There are numerous avenues for publishing tax pieces. Longer and more theoretical papers will likely be published in law reviews. Allen Madison, author of "The Tension Between Textualism and Substance-Over-Form Doctrines in Tax Law," published his piece in the Santa Clara Law Review.

Publishing shorter pieces geared to tax practitioners and business consumers alike is another good way to highlight your tax knowledge. Many of these opportunities to publish shorter, more practical pieces are in tax-related periodicals and magazines, but some are in general legal media like local bar association magazines. These pieces are usually three to four pages long and discuss a current issue in a particular area of tax law. "Publishing is a wonderful way to get your name out there," says Professor Boise. "It shows both your colleagues and potential clients your expertise in a particular area." Some tax attorneys tackle an entire area of tax law by publishing a book. Books and treatises, however, are generally written by experienced attorneys who have already developed a name for themselves in a particular area of law.

Public speaking on panels at tax conferences and meetings is another excellent way to increase your exposure and marketability. These opportunities are normally available to experienced attorneys only, but there are some venues for younger lawyers to get public speaking experience. For example, the Young Lawyers Forum of the American Bar Association Tax Section tries to match interested young attorneys with substantive tax committees. Often the young attorney will have the opportunity to work on substantive, cutting-edge projects, such as comments to proposed regulations. When there is a panel to discuss these proposed regulations the attorney is then in a good position to be one of the presenters.

Keeping up-to-date

Keeping up with current tax and business news is extremely important to demonstrate your interest and commitment to tax. Excellent sources for information in the tax world are in BNA's *Daily Tax Report* and Tax Analysts' *Tax Notes Today*. Most practitioners begin their workday by reading one of these periodicals. Both periodicals can be found on search services like LexisNexis and Westlaw. In addition, it is important to stay up on current business news and trends. Great sources for this information include *The Wall Street Journal*, *Harvard Business Review* and *BusinessWeek*, just to name a few. Finally, once you choose a tax specialty, there are various organizations and associations that can help you stay up on pertinent tax news for your area. For example, the Council On State Taxation (COST) focuses on state and local tax issues and sends weekly e-mail updates to its members about state and local tax news. See Appendix for a list of other resources.

Networking

Sometimes it's not what you know but whom you know. This is true for most professions and tax law is no exception. John O'Neill, director of TaxTalent.com, reminds law students to make use of their contacts when looking for a job. "The hiring process is very important," he says. "This is where using professors, adjunct professors, placement offices, alumni lists, internships or clerkships, and so on, for networking is crucial. A tax person needs to have a little salesman in them to keep persistent in this market." Even experienced lawyers should work on their sales skills. As O'Neill observes, "Networking also helps even the most experienced tax professional. At this level, the professional may belong to an association or two. Also, if they work for a law or accounting firm, they have clients that they can network through."

Many job opportunities are never even posted. Word of mouth and whom you know can often lead to a new position. It is therefore important to build and maintain a good network of contacts. Mildeen Worrell, a tax attorney for the House Ways and Means Committee, advises those seeking congressional jobs to actively network. "Positions on the Hill are rarely advertised outside the Hill community," she says. "Very often, these positions are filled by word of mouth and personal references. Getting to know people who work in your desired environment, and making sure they know of your desire to find a job there must be seriously pursued. Perseverance is a must."

A good place to network is through bar associations. Melinda Merk, former chair of the American Bar Association Tax Section's Young Lawyers Forum, believes that "the ABA is one of the best places for a new lawyer to network with experienced tax professionals. The Young Lawyers Forum hosts a cocktail reception at each Tax Section meeting designed to help new lawyers network. We also help new lawyers get involved with the section's various committees, where they can not only meet other tax professionals but also work on cutting-edge tax issues." Law students can join the ABA Tax Section for free and attend their first ABA Tax Section conference at no cost.

The Young Lawyers Forum also sponsors a tax law competition for law students – a sort of moot court for those students interested in tax law. Accredited ABA law schools are eligible to apply for this competition. Teams of two law students from the same law school, who are advised by a faculty advisor or practicing attorney, first submit a written answer to a fictional tax problem. This problem can be found on the ABA Tax Section's web site and is usually posted sometime in the fall of each year. The response to the problem must be submitted in the form of a memorandum to a senior partner and a letter to a client explaining the team's position on the issue. Six teams are then chosen as semi-finalists to compete in the oral part of the competition, which is generally held at the Tax Section's mid-year meeting. The teams, along with their coaches, receive free round-trip airline tickets and hotel accommodations for two nights for the competition. The six teams present their answers to a group of judges comprised of some of the biggest names in tax, from senior partners to top government officials. The first-place winners receive free membership in the ABA Tax Section and free registration to ABA Tax Section meetings for three years after their graduation.

Local bar associations can also provide opportunities to meet experienced tax attorneys. Many bar associations have active tax committees. For example, the Washington, D.C., Bar Association has a tax section with 10 subcommittees focusing on many tax specialties like corporate, employee benefits, estate planning, exempt organizations, financial products, international tax, pass-throughs and real estate, state and local taxes, tax audits and litigation. Case Law School Professor Boise says, "I found my experience as chair of my local bar association's tax committee an important component of my development as a tax lawyer. I was able to forge valuable relationships with more experienced tax practitioners in the community."

In addition to networking with experienced tax attorneys through such avenues as bar associations, the importance of finding a mentor cannot be overstated. Mildeen Worrell praises her longtime mentor: "I was fortunate enough to clerk on the Tax Court with a wonderful judge – the Hon. Judge Joel Gerber. He taught me so much and I'm proud to call him my mentor. He has helped me at every step of the way during my legal career. In fact, I don't make a decision that impacts my professional career unless I discuss it with him first."

How does a new lawyer find a mentor? Some develop natural relationships on the job or by attending conferences and events. Fortunately, there are also organizations with formal mentorship programs in the tax field. The ABA Tax Section's Diversity Committee is in the process of starting a mentorship program to pair young lawyers with experienced tax attorneys who are active in the Tax Section. In addition, TaxTalent.com sponsors a mentorship program, whereby you can find a mentor online by searching through biographies. Mentors can be chosen based a multitude of criteria such as education, career experience, technical specialty and geographical location.

Interview Tips

With luck and perseverance, the day will arrive when you interview for that perfect job. Interviews can be long monologues or engaging conversations. Since the average interview lasts about 30 minutes, it is important to make a great impression in a short time. You should be prepared for the kinds of questions the interviewer is likely to ask and know something about the organization.

Researching the employer is crucial in preparing for an interview. It is important that the interviewee have a basic understanding of what the organization does prior to the interview. IRS lawyer Shelia Dansby Harvey explains, "So many people who interview with us don't take the time to find out exactly what we do. For example, in Chief Counsel's Office we don't perform audits! Other than meeting statute deadlines, we're not busier on March 15, April 15 and so on, than we are at other times of the year. Not knowing what Chief Counsel does is an immediate turn-off because it tells the interviewer that the applicant isn't interested in the interviewer as an individual and also isn't interested in the job. A job applicant should visit our web site and find out what Chief Counsel does."

Similarly, when interviewing at an accounting firm, it is important to understand that tax attorneys may be asked to prepare tax returns (e.g., compliance work). As Melinda Merk, a tax manager at an accounting firm, observes, "Obviously, a lawyer has to be comfortable with the fact that they are not going to be practicing law/giving legal advice while employed by an accounting firm." In interviews with corporations, the interviewee should have an understanding of the corporation's industry and products or services. It is also important to show that you can function in a team environment. Randle Pollard, tax counsel with a pharmaceutical company, advises candidates to "expect questions that will ask for examples of your leadership ability (e.g., how you perform on a team, deal with difficult team members, clients, and so on). Corporations are looking for individuals who are leaders." "Of course," he adds, "be prepared to answer substantive questions regarding your particular area of expertise in tax law, too."

In preparing for interviews with law firms, understanding the kind of tax that the law firm specializes in is crucial. "Interviewing with a law firm that is known for international tax when your interest is in exempt organization tax is a waste of your time," notes an East Coast lawyer. Most law firms have web sites that discuss their services and clients and provide biographies of their attorneys. From these biographies you can learn a lot about the firm's tax practice and its clients. Being able to articulate your knowledge during the interview will demonstrate that you are serious about the position and genuinely interested in this law firm.

Although preparation is important, in the end, conveying your experiences and interest is the true goal of the interview. Pete Lowy, in-house tax attorney with a large corporation, cautions, "Interviews shouldn't require much preparation just for the sake of the interview. Presumably you have a good reason for applying for the position in the first place, so you should be prepared to answer questions about why you are interested in that company, in that city and doing that type of work. Just be yourself and answer candidly." Fenwick & West associate Allen Madison adds, "People should be prepared to say how they know they like tax rather than other subject areas. Interviewees should think hard about their answer. "

The following questions are among those that might be asked in a typical tax job interview:

- Why are you interested in tax law and what type of tax work are you interested in?

- Why are you interested in this organization?

- Describe some experiences/projects in tax law that you have worked on.

- Describe why you think your skill set/experiences make you a good candidate for this position.

- Where do you see yourself in five years? Ten years?

- Are you a team player or do you prefer to work alone?

- How would you research/handle this project (with the interviewer giving you a sample issue or project)?

- Describe your leadership skills.

There always comes a time in the interview when the interviewer asks, "So do you have any questions for me?" or "What else can I tell you about this organization?" You must be prepared for this. The interviewer is likely trying to gauge your interest in the position and the organization, but this is also an excellent opportunity for you to find out more about the organization and whether or not you would like to work there. Think about what you want in a job and whether this particular employer will meet your needs. Consider posing the following questions:

- What skill sets are most important to be successful in this position?

- Why did you choose tax as a profession?

- What type of training or mentorship does your firm/company provide and will I have an opportunity to work directly with senior tax attorneys?

- Will I get direct client contact?

- What was the most challenging tax project that you have worked on and how did you overcome this challenge?

- Describe a typical day for you.

- After working in this position for a few years, which skill sets do you think I will have gained? Were do you see this position leading in five or ten years?

- Would you describe the work environment as team-oriented or individualistic?

Cover Letters, Resumes and Addenda

CHAPTER 10

On top of job searches, networking and employer research, there is another essential aspect to landing that perfect job: a good cover letter, resume and addendum.

The Cover Letter

A cover letter is your first opportunity to introduce yourself and your accomplishments to a prospective employer. According to John O'Neill, "Cover letters should not come across as a heavy sales pitch of your background. It is important not to oversell yourself. Instead they should let the potential employer know that you have an interest in the position and that there needs to be further exploration on the part of both parties."

O'Neill warns, however, "A cover letter should not be generic. Stay away from phrases like 'I would be a great asset to your company.' Also, make the letter specific to the company and the position and be sure to make reference to anything you have done that matches what they need. Finally, I cannot stress this enough, make sure that your cover letter looks professional and is error free. If mailing it, make sure the paper is of a nice stock, neat without smudges and of course no typos. The same holds true for e-mailed cover letters. If e-mailing the cover letter make sure you have saved the document using a professional name like JohnDoecoverletter.doc. Stay away from using cutesy names. Treat your cover letter like an in-person interview. After all, no one would go to an interview with a pair of dirty sneakers on – that is what a bad cover letter is like."

TaxTalent.com's web site suggests that a cover letter should include the following elements:

- How the job description matches your tax background.

- Why you are interested in this position. Reasons might include the kind of tax work or the job's location.

- Express interest in further exploring whether the opportunity would be a good match from both your and the employer's perspectives.

Your Resume

A resume should give a truthful overview of your professional life. At a minimum, it should cover your educational achievements, professional work experience and accomplishments, and professional activities. In the words of TaxTalent.com's John O'Neill, "A resume should always tell the truth and give the sense of what you have done. If a company or firm that you worked for is a non-Fortune 500 corporation, explain what it is on the resume (i.e., ABC Company, $50 million manufacturing firm)." O'Neill adds that, for those still in law school or recent graduates with little previous work experience, "resumes should have more information on leadership activities."

According to TaxTalent.com, a resume should include the following elements:

- **EDUCATION.** List each school, degree, year of degree completion, honors, GPA and/or class ranking.

- **CERTIFICATIONS.** Include CPA, bar memberships and the like.

- **WORK HISTORY.** List all positions in chronological order with the most recent at the top. Each position should include:

  - **EMPLOYER.** Under the employer name, include two or three sentences describing the company: revenue size, industry type, short description of international structure. (For example: $5 billion pharmaceutical company with operations in Europe, Asia and Latin America including 10 manufacturing sites and 20 distribution centers outside the U.S.) It is not necessary to include a company description for a Big Four public accounting firm or major law firm.

  - **JOB TITLE**

  - **DATES OF EMPLOYMENT.** List all positions and dates of employment. If you have had multiple positions at one employer, first provide the overall dates and then list the specific dates for each position.

  - **JOB DESCRIPTION** (one paragraph for each position). Describe your role and major areas of responsibility. Include the reporting structure – whom you report to and who reports to you. Keep first-person references to a minimum. You want to bring across your abilities as a team player.

  - **ADDITIONAL SECTIONS** at the end of your resume can include publications, professional organizations (e.g., Tax Executives Institute,

American Bar Association), computer skills and personal accomplishments, but keep these short.

It is not necessary to include a career objectives/career summary description or to list references (you can provide those when you are actively in the process of interviewing).

- **RESUME NAME.** When saving your resume as a Word (or other word processing software) document, use your name. Human resource and tax hiring professionals receive many resumes each day called "Resume.doc" or something equally generic. The best way to have your resume properly noticed and categorized is by calling it something like JohnSmithTaxResume.doc or JaneDoeTaxAttorney.doc.

The resume should be printed on a nice stock of white paper; don't use unusual colors. A professional typeface like Times Roman should be used and font size should not be less than 10 point. With TaxTalent.com's resume template, called the TaxTalent Resume Builder, you can develop your resume online and have it posted for prospective employers to review.

The Addendum

In recent years, addenda to resumes have become popular as a way to convey more on-point information about an applicant's qualifications. According to TaxTalent.com, addenda should be one to three pages long and list all of your pertinent accomplishments using bullet points.

"Addenda should be specific to the position and to the company," says John O'Neill. "This is where you take your experience at ABC Company and relate it to what you know about the position that you are applying for. So, if you are applying for an international tax position and worked on some projects that are pertinent, your addendum might describe one of your projects like, 'Worked on permanent establishment issues in four countries where no business had been previously conducted.'"

An addendum should include:

- Technical projects and/or examples of leadership/management accomplishments

- Quantification of tax-technical accomplishments (e.g., approximate dollars saved, approximate liability exposure avoided in dollars, percentage reduction in the effective tax rate, increased cash flow by so many dollars)

- A section listing projects from your current employer and additional section(s) listing projects from past employers. Include projects that directly relate to the position under consideration.

Sample Cover Letters, Resumes and Addenda

The following sample cover letters, resumes and addenda are provided for three fictional tax attorneys. Please note the following samples are purely fictional.

John Taxwannabee

Mr. Taxwannabee is a recent graduate of the University of Richmond School of Law. As an undergraduate at the University of Michigan, John had no idea that he would end up in law school. He majored in psychology and thought that he might pursue a Ph.D. But by his senior year he was burned out from studying and decided to postpone getting another degree. He got a job in corporate America working as a public relations specialist. John enjoyed this position because he got to work directly with people, the main reason he chose to major in psychology. But after several years of working he decided that if he wanted to advance he would need a graduate degree.

By now he looked forward to being in school for a few years. He had always been interested in business, so at first he thought about pursuing an MBA. However, in his role as a public relations specialist, he dealt with a lot of politicians and legislators and really liked the public policy aspect of his job. So he thought that law school would make more sense. Once in law school, John thought he would go into either litigation or corporate law. After doing a summer clerkship, however, John decided that his real interests were in the tax field. When he returned to law school for his third year, he was determined to obtain a position in the tax profession.

JOHN TAXWANNABEE
1234 ANYSTREET, ANYTOWN USA 12345
(202) 123-4567 • Ilovetax@hotmail.com

September 1, 2003

ABC Law Firm
1234 Main Street
Washington, D.C., 20000

Re: Tax Associate Position

Ladies and Gentlemen:

Enclosed is a recent copy of my resume and addendum. I respectfully request that you consider my background in choosing an individual for the position of tax associate dealing with controversy matters. I have experience in the area of tax controversy and thoroughly enjoy this practice area. My time with the University of Richmond Law Tax Clinic provided me with the opportunity to gain hands-on experience in dealing with clients and in negotiating settlements with the IRS. I also developed significant research and writing skills in advocating my client's position.

I'm very interested in your tax associate position because I believe it will afford me the opportunity both to apply my advocating skills and to grow as a professional. Moreover, I am originally from the Washington, D.C., area and am very interested in returning to the region to continue my practice.

I would like the opportunity to present my credentials to you personally. If you care to speak with me directly, you can contact me at 123-456-7890 (office) or 202-123-4567 (home). I look forward to further exploring whether this opportunity would be a good match from both our perspectives.

Sincerely,

John Taxwannabee

Enclosures

Vault Guide to Tax Law Careers
Cover Letter, Resumes and Addenda

JOHN TAXWANNABEE
1234 ANYSTREET, ANYTOWN USA 12345
(202) 123-4567 • ILOVETAX@HOTMAIL.COM

> This e-mail address is too cutesy. He should use a professional e-mail address like johntaxwannabee@hotmail.com

EDUCATION

University of Richmond School of Law, JD, May 2003

> John may want to consider an LL.M. Because he did not go to a top-25 law school, nor was he at the top of his class, an LL.M from a top-three program may be the most helpful.

University of Michigan, Ann Arbor, BS in Psychology, May 1996

BAR ADMISSIONS

Sat for the July 2003 Virginia Bar Exam

EXPERIENCE

University of Richmond Law Tax Clinic, Richmond, Va. Student Attorney (2002-2003)

> This prior work experience is good in showing an interest in tax, particularly for a tax controversy position. However, it may not be that helpful for certain tax specialties like corporate tax, international tax or estate planning.

Represented taxpayers in federal tax controversy disputes. Researched various federal tax issues. Prepared, wrote and reviewed private letter ruling requests and other IRS legal and administrative memoranda. Observed U.S. Tax Court proceedings. Participated in taxpayer outreach forums.

Wonderful & Wonderful, LLP, Burke, Va. Summer Associate (2002)

Clerked as a summer associate in the litigation group and the corporate group. Also drafted research memoranda for tax partner dealing with various tax transactions for partnerships.

Virginia Commonwealth University, Business Department, Richmond, Va. Teaching Assistant (2000-2002)

Taught 200 undergraduate students in business law course. Researched and analyzed various business law issues for professor's book, Teaching Business Law.

ABDC Insurance Company, Philadelphia, Pa. Public Affairs Specialist (1997-2000)

Responsible for coordinating all company public affairs events in Pennsylvania, Delaware and New Jersey. Drafted press releases on public affair events and worked closely with the Vice President of Communications on strategic planning for upcoming public affair events.

University of Michigan, Admissions Office, Ann Arbor, Mich. Assistant to Dean of Admissions (1996-1997)

Served as assistant to the Dean of Admissions. Set up an electronic database to keep track of applications and responses to applications.

PROFESSIONAL ORGANIZATIONS & ACTIVITIES

> To bolster a fresh grad's resume, volunteer work and leadership roles are important.

Volunteer Income Tax Assistant Program, Site Coordinator for the University of Richmond
American Bar Association Section of Taxation
University of Michigan Alumni Association, President, Class of 1996

Addendum

JOHN TAXWANNABEE
1234 ANYSTREET, ANYTOWN USA 12345
(202) 123-4567 • Ilovetax@hotmail.com

UNIVERSITY OF RICHMOND LAW TAX CLINIC

- Handled 50 offer and compromises for clients in front of the IRS.
- Saved a client over $500,000 in federal taxes.
- Negotiated favorable settlements of over $2 million for clients.
- Trained three law students to handle client cases.
- Developed case management computer database to track the status of cases.

> This position helps to demonstrate John's interest in tax and would likely be extremely helpful if John is interested doing controversy work.

VOLUNTEER INCOME TAX ASSISTANT PROGRAM

- Coordinated the entire tax return preparation site.
- Supervised over 50 volunteers who prepared returns.
- Handled and prepared over 200 federal tax returns.
- Reviewed over 500 federal tax returns.
- Received up-to-date training from the IRS.

> This work with VITA also shows John has a real interest in tax even though he may not have majored in accounting or had many positions in the tax field. It also shows he has leadership skills. This should help to set him apart from other candidates and may be particularly helpful if he is applying for a job with the IRS or for a compliance position with an accounting firm or a corporation.

Jane Taxhopeful

Ms. Taxhopeful is a recent graduate of Stanford University Law School. She graduated from Pepperdine University where she majored in business administration. After college she worked with a big corporation as an accounting clerk. She often interacted with the company's tax department and found their work very interesting. She also enjoyed the two tax classes she took while in college. But she knew that she would need a graduate degree if she was going to be an attractive candidate for the tax department. At first she considered getting a master's degree in taxation. But she'd always been interested in law school and spoke to the tax director of her company who advised her to consider becoming a tax attorney. Jane entered law school with the objective of becoming a tax attorney. She focused all of her coursework, as well as her job experiences, in the tax field.

JANE TAXHOPEFUL
1234 CLIFFORD ST, LOS ANGELES, CA 90012
(987) 654-3210 • Janetaxhopeful@hotmail.com

September 1, 2003

DEF Law Firm
1234 Main Street
San Francisco, CA, 20000

Re: Tax Associate – Estate Planning Group

Ladies and Gentlemen:

Enclosed is a recent copy of my resume. I respectfully request that you consider my background in choosing an individual for the position of Tax Associate in your Estate Planning Group.

As my resume indicates, I'm a recent graduate of Stanford University Law School and I have held several positions in the tax field. These positions have given me exposure to a wide range of tax issues including partnership tax, corporate tax, estate planning, exempt organizations, and state and local tax.

My interest in tax began when I was a senior accounting associate with a Fortune 500 corporation and my position required that I interact frequently with the tax department. It is this interest that led me to law school where I focused on taxation courses and took 10 tax classes (in both the law school and the business school).

I'm very interested in your Tax Associate position because I'm interested in estate planning issues. I worked on several estate planning projects during my summer clerkship. Moreover, I believe my other experiences, like drafting partnership agreements, are valuable and overlap in the estate planning area.

I would like the opportunity to present my credentials to you personally. If you care to speak with me directly, you can contact me at 123-456-7890 (office) or 987-654-3210 (home).

Sincerely,

Jane Taxhopeful

Enclosure

> Jane's experiences show that she has not specialized in any one area of tax. She has done many things like partnerships, corporate, exempt organizations, state and local tax and some estate planning. As a new law school graduate, this is good because it makes her an attractive candidate to numerous organizations. She can be molded into whatever specialty that the organization is seeking.

Jane Taxhopeful
1234 Clifford St. • Los Angeles, CA 90012 • (987) 654-3210
Email: Janetaxhopeful@hotmail.com

Education

STANFORD UNIVERSITY LAW SCHOOL, J.D., MAY 2002
Honors: Ranked in the top 20 percent of the class
Activities: Volunteered with the San Francisco Tax Law Clinic to represent indigent clients with tax issues

PEPPERDINE UNIVERSITY, B.S., BUSINESS ADMINISTRATION, MAY 1994
Cumulative GPA: 3.75/4.00

Experience

MEGA BIG LAW FIRM — *San Francisco, California*
Summer Associate — *(May 2001-August 2001)*

Tax practice included partnerships, trusts and estates, nonprofit organization tax matters, estate tax, and corporate mergers and acquisitions. Activities involved research and writing legal memoranda and partnership agreements, advising exempt organizations on obtaining and maintaining tax-exempt status, structuring and analyzing sophisticated wealth transfer tax transactions, analyzing corporate restructurings, and responding to IRS information document requests.

PROFESSOR ALAN I. KNOWTAX — *San Francisco, California*
Research Assistant — *(September 2000-May 2001)*

Worked as a student assistant to a tax professor researching issues affecting low-income housing tax credits. My research will be used in writing his upcoming book on the subject.

FINAL FOUR ACCOUNTING FIRM — *San Francisco, California*
Summer Associate — *(May 2000-August 2000)*

Researched and analyzed state and local tax issues for multistate corporations. Issues included apportionment formulas, nexus concerns and compliance procedures. Drafted memoranda and protest letters to various state agencies. Analyzed clients' financial documents and restructured transactions in preparation for federal and state tax return files.

XYZ CORP — *Los Angeles, California*
Senior Accounting Associate — *(September 1994-May 1999)*

Responsible for accounting issues regarding the company's property plant and equipment account. Interacted regularly with the tax and the finance departments on the correct accounting treatment of various properties. Ran depreciation reports and was in charge of reconciling total depreciation on an annual basis. Managed a team of three accounting analysts.

ADDENDUM
Jane Taxhopeful

> Jane's examples are good but she may want to break them out by position so that a prospective employer can get a better feel for what she did in her various jobs.

Examples of Accomplishments

- Drafted protests to five state taxing authorities advocating the client's position. Won in four out of the five matters, saving the client over $2 million in taxes.

- Filed 10 exemption applications for nonprofits (Form 1023) and received unanimous approval on all applications.

- Helped indigent client who hadn't filed tax returns in 10 years and spoke little English reach an agreement with the IRS whereby after applying earned income tax credits she received a $10,000 refund from the IRS.

- Drafted 20 partnership agreements for a transaction involving the merger of two closely held family businesses.

- Wrote memorandum on the optimal method to accomplish a corporate reorganization. My recommendation of a forward triangular merger was used as a basis for the client letter sent by a senior partner with my memorandum attached as backup for the position.

- Assisted senior partner in analyzing the estate and gift tax impact of a contemplated transfer of the assets of a closely held business to the next generation. Drafted wills and reviewed estate tax returns for this same partner.

- Researched the tax implications of exercising incentive stock options for high-net-worth individuals who were executives at a major corporation.

- Assisted client, a medium-sized manufacturing company, in responding to over 100 information document requests from the IRS.

Joanna Taxpert

Joanna Taxpert has been practicing as a tax attorney with a big law firm for five years. She has enjoyed working for a law firm, but has decided for lifestyle and family reasons to consider a different position. She is open to a position with a corporation, the government or an accounting firm. Her only requirement is that the job allow her to continue specializing in international tax.

JOANNA TAXPERT
2300 TAX ALLEY, WASHINGTON DC 20006
(202) 777-9311 • jtaxpert@hotmail.com

September 1, 2003

XYZ Corporation
555 Corporate Row
Washington, D.C. 20000

Re: International Manager Position

Dear Recruiter:

I was pleased to see the posting of the International Tax Manager opportunity on the TaxTalent.com web site. I'm enclosing a copy of my resume and addendum for your consideration.

As outlined on my resume, I hold an LL.M in Taxation and have five years of tax experience. All of my legal experiences have been with law firms, where I have focused on international tax issues. Prior to becoming a lawyer, I worked in the international finance group for a Fortune 500 company.

I'm intrigued by the opportunity to work with another Fortune 500 company in the international arena. I believe it will afford me the opportunity to apply my legal planning skills and at the same time exploit my corporate finance skills. Also, because of these experiences, I'm very comfortable dealing with financial and non-financial individuals alike. As your position requires someone who can effectively communicate sophisticated and technical international tax issues to other managers in the company, I believe that I'm uniquely qualified for this role.

I'm very interested in pursuing this opportunity with you further. I can be reached during working hours at 202-444-1234. I look forward to further exploring whether this opportunity would be a good match from both our perspectives. Thank you for your consideration.

Sincerely,

Joanna Taxpert

Enclosure

JOANNA TAXPERT
2300 Tax Alley Washington DC 20006
Work (202) 444-1234 Home (202) 777-9311
jtaxpert@hotmail.com

[Annotation: Good professional e-mail address.]

EDUCATION

GEORGETOWN UNIVERSITY, Washington, DC
LL.M. in Taxation, May 1998
- 6th in class

[Annotation: Good educational background. Some may argue that Joanna did not need an LL.M. Nevertheless, with this background it is clear that she has an interest in tax law.]

UNIVERSITY OF VIRGINIA SCHOOL OF LAW, Charlottesville, VA
J.D., May 1997
- Virginia Tax Review
- Top 15 percent of class

UNIVERSITY OF MICHIGAN, Ann Arbor, MI
B.S. in Accounting, May 1990

EXPERIENCE

REALLY BIG LAW FIRM, Washington, DC
Associate: Summers 1996 and 1997, September 1998-present

[Annotation: Excellent work experiences in private industry and the government – all showing her interest in tax and specifically in the international area.]

Practice in the international tax group. Activities include counseling clients on myriad international tax issues including Subpart F income, Section 936 possessions corporations, cross-border mergers and acquisitions, foreign sales corporation and extraterritorial income issues, foreign tax credits, preeminent establishment issues, international migration of intangibles, corporate inversion techniques and commissionaire/principal structures.

INTERNAL REVENUE SERVICE, Washington, DC
Clerk: Winter 1996 and Spring 1997

Clerked in the IRS National Office, International Branch. Researched and drafted legal memoranda for revenue rulings, private letter rulings and various other IRS correspondence. Received intensive training in tax research and the inter-workings of the National Office of the Internal Revenue Service. Received class credit for this experience.

RIVAL TO REALLY BIG LAW FIRM, Washington, DC
Associate: Summer 1995

Researched and drafted memorandum on transfer pricing issues affecting several multinational companies. Reviewed treaties with several countries to help clients minimize foreign income taxes. Worked with senior partner on gathering and reviewing various studies used to help clients in meeting their U.S. and foreign transfer pricing documentation requirements.

SUPER BIG CORPORATION, Washington, DC
Senior Financial Analyst: September 1990-July 1994

Worked as a senior analyst in the corporate international finance department. Responsibilities included developing financial models to be used by various corporate departments such as tax, accounting and the licensing group.

Resume of Joanna Taxpert
Page 2

BAR ADMISSION

- Member of the Bar of the District of Columbia

SPEECHES AND PUBLICATIONS

- Author, "International Tax Issues for the Ex-Patriot," *A General Business Magazine*, June 12, 2003

- Speech, "Section 904 FTC – What Does it Really Mean?" Local Bar Association Tax Section Summer Meeting, June 2003

- Speech, "EIT, A New Solution to an Age Old Problem," Local Bar Association Tax Section Winter Meeting, December 2002

- Co-author, "The Proposed Section 367(b) Regulations," *An International Tax Journal* (June 2001)

- Author, "Setting up a Principal/Commissionaire Structure," *An International Tax Journal* (November 2000)

- Speech, "The New Age for Foreign Sales Corporations," An International Tax Seminar, May 2000

- Author, " International Tax and E-Commerce Issues," *A Tax Law Review* (May 1998)

PROFESSIONAL ASSOCIATIONS

- American Bar Association, Section of Taxation
- Washington, DC Bar Tax Section

Speeches and publications are a great way to market yourself. Joanna is showing that she is really developing an expertise in the international tax area. Notice that her first publication, which is often the hardest, was a law review piece and was likely done for school credit while she was getting her LL.M. After working for a while and building a name for herself, her most recent piece is in a general business magazine.

Addendum of Joanna Taxpert

> Good list overall, but Joanna should try to add a little more detail to some of her bullet points – like an example of how she minimized the tax exposure. Of course, she must do so without giving away the client or the exact details of the transaction.

> Good to quantify how much you saved or helped he client.

REALLY BIG LAW FIRM

- Served as project manager on an issue for client to minimize foreign source income. Team included cross-functional members from client's accounting, finance and operations department.

- Assisted client in maximizing foreign sales corporation benefit by $10 million per year.

- Developed and structured Section 956 repatriation strategies for six clients.

- Assisted client in minimizing exposure of foreign income taxes.

- Reviewed transfer pricing reports prepared by economists and assisted clients in complying with U.S. transfer-pricing contemporaneous documentation requirements.

- Helped client, a foreign parent, repatriate cash from several U.S. subsidiaries in a tax-efficient manner.

- Assisted five clients in evaluating and setting up commissionaires and principals in several European countries.

SUPER BIG CORPORATION

- Led in-house corporate team in evaluating various financing structures to be used in the purchase of a European company.

- Served as the point person in international finance for the corporate licensing group. Ran numerous financial models for international licensing deals.

- Presented quarterly PowerPoint presentations to senior management on status of international portfolio.

- Managed a staff of five junior financial analysts.

APPENDIX

The following appendix provides:

- A list of top tax law firms
- Organizations and resources geared to tax professionals, federal agencies and courts that handle tax matters
- News and research services providing the latest tax information.

This is by no means an exhaustive list, but it includes some of the most common resources.

Top Tax Law Firms

Most major law firms have sizeable tax departments. Even medium-sized law firms usually have several tax lawyers. But, as with most things in life, there are those that stand head and shoulders above the rest. Some law firms rank high nationally, while others are the best in their region. For the truly top tax law firms with global operations, the list is short.

Chambers and Partners (www.chambersandpartners.com), a leader in publishing world-famous guides to the legal profession, crowned international law firm, Cleary, Gottlieb, Steen & Hamilton (www.cgsh.com), the American tax law firm of the year for 2003. Runners-up were the New York-based Davis Polk & Wardwell (www.dpw.com) and McKee Nelson LLP (http://mneylaw.com), an independent law firm allied with Ernst & Young.

Other notable law firms with top tax practices include:

New York
Cravath Swaine & Moore LLP (www.cravath.com)

Boston
Ropes & Gray LLP (www.ropesgray.com)
Hale and Dorr LLP* (www.haledorr.com)
Goodwin Procter LLP (www.goodwinprocter.com)
(Soon to be Wilmer Cutler Pickering Hale and Dorr LLP, www.wilmerhale.com)

Washington, D.C.
Caplin & Drysdale (www.capdale.com)

Atlanta
Sutherland Asbill & Brennan LLP (www.sablaw.com)
Alston & Bird LLP (www.alston.com)

Florida
Dean Mead (www.deanmead.com)
Greenberg Traurig, LLP (www.gtlaw.com)
Holland & Knight LLP (www.hklaw.com)
Steel Hector & Davis LLP (www.steelhector.com)

Texas
Vinson & Elkins L.L.P. (www.vinson-elkins.com)

Chicago
Kirkland & Ellis LLP (www.kirkland.com)

Mayer, Brown, Rowe & Maw LLP (www.mayerbrownrowe.com)

California
Irell & Manella LLP (www.irell.com)
Latham & Watkins LLP (www.lw.com)

Industry Organizations and Resources

There are many organizations that cater to tax professionals. Some are narrowly defined and seek to serve tax subspecialties. Others are aimed at the tax profession as a whole. The following is an overview of some of the tax organizations and resources for tax professionals.

ALI-ABA

American Law Institute – American Bar Association (ALI-ABA) is the result of a collaborative, nonprofit endeavor between the American Bar Association and the American Law Institute to organize a national program of continuing professional education classes for lawyers. ALI-ABA offers tax seminars on a wide range of substantive subjects. For more information visit their web site at www.ali-aba.org.

Alliance for Tax, Legal and Accounting Seminars

Alliance for Tax, Legal and Accounting Seminars (ATLAS), affiliated with ATLAS-SFI Information Group, offers numerous tax courses of interest to companies doing business overseas or cross-border and covers topics such as U.S.-international taxation and the taxation of financial products. These courses are held throughout the United States, with basic to advanced level seminars. For more information visit their web site at www.atlas-sfi.com.

American Bar Association Section of Taxation

The American Bar Association is the largest voluntary professional association in the world. It has more than 400,000 members and among the many services it offers members are continuing legal education classes. The ABA has over 22 sections divided by substantive areas of law, including a tax section. The Section of Taxation has approximately 20,000 members nationwide. In addition to continuing education programs offered throughout the year in various locations, the Section of Taxation holds three meetings a year, including its annual May meeting in Washington, D.C. Membership is open to attorneys and law students. For more information visit their web site at www.abanet.org/tax.

American College of Trust and Estate Counsel

The American College of Trust and Estate Counsel is an association of lawyers experienced in the preparation of wills and trusts, estate planning, probate procedure, and administration of trusts and estates of decedents. The college has approximately 2,700 members throughout the United States. The members of the college, known as fellows, nominate new members. For more information visit their web site at www.actec.org.

American Institute of Certified Public Accountants

The American Institute of Certified Public Accountants (AICPA), with over 336,000 members, is the largest professional organization in the country serving CPAs. Regular membership is open only to certified public accountants. The AICPA also has a Tax Section with over 24,000 members who focus on tax matters. Student membership is open to students as early as their freshman year all the way through graduate school. A non-CPA membership is available in the Tax Division to non-CPA professionals employed and sponsored by a CPA firm (e.g., attorneys working at CPA firms). For more information, visit their web site at www.aicpa.org.

American Society of Women Accountants

The American Society of Women Accountants (ASWA) is a professional organization for women who practice in accounting, finance and related professions. ASWA has chapters throughout the United States and holds a national conference. Members include partners in national, regional and local CPA firms; financial officers; controllers; academics; financial analysts and data processing consultants; recent college graduates and women returning to the work force. Regular membership is open to CPAs who have been practicing in accounting for at least two years, while affiliate membership is open to all who have a substantial interest in accounting. Student memberships are available to regularly enrolled students with fewer than two years experience in accounting. For more information visit their web site at www.aswa.org.

American Taxation Association

The American Taxation Association is a section of a larger organization, the American Accounting Association. ATA is a service designed to promote tax education, research and practice. Membership is open to persons with an interest in tax education and research; most members work in academia. It is also open to full-time students. For more information visit their web site at www.atasection.org.

Association of Corporate Counsel

The Association of Corporate Counsel (ACC) – formerly known as the American Corporate Counsel Association, or ACCA – is geared toward attorneys practicing in-house with corporations and other private sector organizations. Known as ACC America in the United States, the organization has over 14,000 members representing 6,500 corporations in 40 countries, with 43 chapters and 12 committees serving the membership. Its members represent 49 of the Fortune 50 companies and 97 of the Fortune 100 companies. Internationally, ACC members represent 42 of the Global 50 and 77 of the Global 100 companies.

In addition to continuing legal education classes, ACC offers a job search service on its web site for in-house positions throughout the world. Membership is open only to attorneys who practice law as employees of organizations and who do not hold themselves out to the public for the practice of law. For more information, visit their web site at www.acca.com.

Association of Latino Professionals in Finance and Accounting

The Association of Latino Professionals in Finance and Accounting (ALPFA) is a professional organization for Latinos who practice in accounting, finance and related professions. ALPFA has chapters throughout the country that put on their own programs and the association also holds a national conference. To become a member, you must hold a degree in accounting, finance or a related field. For more information visit their web site at www.alpfa.org.

Council for International Tax Education

The Council for International Tax Education, Inc. (CITE) is a nonprofit educational organization and a provider of live and online conferences for corporate tax professionals. CITE focuses on educating U.S. and foreign multinationals and companies engaged in international business on the tax, legal and accounting aspects of doing business overseas and provides members with tax publications, newsletters and educational seminars. Membership is open to individuals and corporations. Non-members may also attend CITE seminars and conferences. For more information visit their web site at www.citeusa.org.

Council On State Taxation

The Council On State Taxation (COST) is a membership organization representing taxpayers and focusing on state tax issues. COST's objective is to preserve and promote equitable and nondiscriminatory state and local taxation of multi-jurisdictional business entities. Membership in COST is only open to corporations. COST has approximately 550 multistate corporations members. Only employees of COST member companies may attend COST conferences and schools. For more information visit their web site at www.statetax.org.

European American Tax Institute

European American Tax Institute (EATI) is open to professionals with an interest in international tax. EATI has over 400 members and sponsors round-table discussions throughout Europe and the United States where professionals can trade creative planning techniques and benchmarking on international tax subjects. EATI also sponsors seminars and courses on many international tax topics. Membership is open to individuals and corporations. Non-members may attend EATI seminars and conferences. For more information visit their web site at www.e-ati.com.

Multistate Tax Commission

The Multistate Tax Commission is a joint agency of state governments formed to improve fairness and efficiency in state tax systems. It is comprised of tax administrators from various states. The commission studies state tax issues and makes recommendations to states to develop uniformity in state tax laws and regulations. For more information visit their web site at www.mtc.gov.

National Association of Black Accountants

The National Association of Black Accountants (NABA) is a professional organization representing the interests of over 100,000 African-Americans and other minorities participating in the fields of accounting, auditing, business, consulting, finance and information technology. Membership is open to professionals and students interested in accounting. NABA sponsors an annual conference and several regional student conferences. For more information visit their web site at www.nabainc.org.

National Bar Association

The National Bar Association (NBA) is the nation's oldest and largest national association of predominately African American lawyers. It has many sections divided by substantive legal areas including a Tax Law Section. Membership is open to practicing attorneys and law students. The NBA sponsors an annual conference and several regional conferences. For more information visit their web site at www.nationalbar.org.

Tax Executives Institute

Tax Executives Institute is a professional organization of corporate business executives responsible for taxation matters on an administrative or policy-making level, or whose work is otherwise primarily concerned with the problems of business taxation. The institute has over 5,300 members, aligned in 53 separate chapters, who represent 2,700 of the leading businesses in the United States, Canada and Europe. Most members are accountants, lawyers and other corporate and business employees who are responsible for the tax affairs of their employers in an executive, administrative or managerial capacity. Membership is only open to tax professionals with five years of corporate tax experience. It is not open to tax professionals in public practice (e.g., law firms or accounting firms). For more information visit their web site at www.tei.org.

TaxSearch

TaxSearch, Inc. is the largest tax recruiting firm in the world whose client list includes many major U.S. companies. It offers searches for tax professionals across a wide range of organizations and corporations. It also helps interested tax professionals locate compatible tax positions. For more information visit their web site at www.taxsearchinc.com.

TaxTalent.com

TaxTalent.com, founded in 1999, is an online career management and resource center devoted exclusively to tax professionals. It offers a free career portal for tax professionals and includes information on career management and counseling, open tax positions, tax training events, a diversity forum, mentors and salaries. For more information visit their web site at www.taxtalent.com.

Federal Agencies and Courts

Internal Revenue Service

The Internal Revenue Service's main web site is located at www.irs.gov. For tax professionals, a section of the site offers helpful information and professional tools on current tax topics and resources for tax preparation. For more on the professional tools visit www.irs.gov/taxpros/index.html.

The IRS also provides a student lessons section with 36 lessons in two content areas: the Hows of Taxes, which focuses on the basics of tax preparation, and the Whys of Taxes, which focuses on understanding taxes, including the history of taxes, what is taxed and why. For more on the student lessons visit www.irs.gov/app/understandingTaxes/jsp/s_student_lessons.jsp.

U.S. Court of Federal Claims

Approximately one-fourth of all cases heard by the Court of Federal Claims involve tax refunds. The court has 16 judges appointed by the president. It is located in Washington, D.C., although judges travel to hear cases in certain cities around the country. For more information visit their web site at www.uscfc.uscourts.gov.

U.S. Department of Justice, Tax Division

The Tax Division represents the IRS in most civil and criminal litigation. The Tax Division employs more than 350 attorneys, most of whom are based in Washington, D.C.

U.S. Department of the Treasury, Office of Tax Policy

The Office of Tax Policy works closely with the IRS in developing tax regulations. For more information on this office visit their web site at www.ustreas.gov/offices/tax-policy.

For more information visit their web site at www.usdoj.gov/tax.

U.S. Tax Court

The United States Tax Court decides tax controversies between taxpayers and the IRS. There are 19 judges on the Tax Court, all appointed by the president. Although the court is located in Washington, D.C., judges also travel to hear cases in certain cities around the country. For more information visit their web site at www.ustaxcourt.gov.

Tax Research and News Services

In addition to legal research on services like **LexisNexis** (www.lexisnexis.com) and **Westlaw** (www.westlaw.com), tax professionals rely on some of the following sources to keep abreast of tax news and events.

BNA Tax Management

BNA, Inc. is one of the best-known publishers of print and electronic news, analysis and reference products covering legal and regulatory devolupments. The BNA Tax Management Library provides in-depth coverage of federal, state and foreign tax, and estate, gifts and trusts topics. Products include various tax management portfolios, the *Daily Tax Report* and several monthly and weekly tax journals and reports. The web site also includes free tax articles and federal and state tax highlights. For more information visit www.bna.com/tm/index.html.

CCH

CCH Incorporated is another major producer of electronic and print tax products. CCH's products cover a range of tax specialties including federal tax, state tax, international tax, real estate tax, excise taxes, financial and estate planning, partnerships, exempt organizations, limited liability companies and S corporations. CCH publishes the *Standard Federal Tax Reporter* and numerous guides, reports and books. On its web site you'll also find updates on current tax news and legislation. CCH's main web site is located at www.cch.com. For information about tax and accounting services, visit http://tax.cchgroup.com.

Chronicle of Philanthropy

The *Chronicle of Philanthropy* calls itself the newspaper of the nonprofit world. The paper's web site contains archived articles on myriad tax issues affecting nonprofit organizations. It also has a searchable job listings database for nonprofit positions throughout the United States. For more information visit its web site at http://philanthropy.com.

Kleinrock

Kleinrock provides tax research and tax compliance products, including the Total Tax Office, a combination of tax compliance and tax research software. Kleinrock also publishes a *Daily Tax Bulletin* and numerous books on various tax subjects. For more information visit its web site at www.kleinrock.com.

Research Institute of America

Research Institute of America (RIA) is a leading provider of tax research tools and practice materials for tax and accounting professionals. RIA publishes the *U.S. Tax Reporter* library, a Code-organized tax reporter, and numerous tax treatises and journals covering topics like federal tax, state tax, corporate tax, exempt organizations, real estate tax, estate planning, business entities and international tax. RIA's web site provides updates on current tax news and legislation as well as sample articles from its various journals. For more information visit its web site at www.riahome.com.

Tax Analysts

Tax Analysts is a nonprofit corporation and a widely known and respected provider of tax magazines, books, databases, CDs and online products. Its products include *Tax Notes Today, State Tax Today, Tax Notes International* and numerous other tax-focused publications which are published daily, weekly and monthly. The publications cover state, federal and international tax laws and issues. According to its web site, Tax Analysts has more reporters and commentators dedicated exclusively to tax issues than any other company. Free daily tax bulletins are available via e-mail. For more information visit its web site at www.taxanalysts.com.

The Tax Prophet

The Tax Prophet, put together by San Francisco solo practitioner Robert L. Sommers, is a free online service that publishes tax articles. Topics are generally narrower than those handled by other tax publications and include such issues as Internet taxation, tax planning for expatriates (U.S. taxpayers working overseas) and taxation of day traders. It also offers tax classes on many subjects. For more information visit the web site at www.taxprophet.com.

VAULT LAW CAREER LIBRARY

You are reading just one title from Vault's Law Career Library - the complete resource for legal careers. To see a full list of legal career titles, go to law.vault.com.

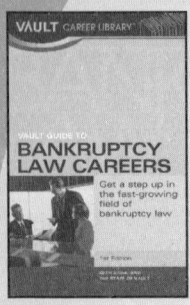

"With reviews and profiles of firms that one associate calls 'spot on,' [Vault's] guide has become a key reference for those who want to know what it takes to get hired by a law firm and what to expect once they get there."

– New York Law Journal

"To get the unvarnished scoop, check out Vault."

– SmartMoney magazine

VAULT
> the most trusted name in career information™

"Vault is indispensable for locating insider information."
- Metropolitan Corporate Counsel

About the Author

Shannon King Nash

Shannon King Nash is a tax attorney practicing in-house with a major Fortune 500 company. Previously, she was a tax associate with the law firm Cooley Godward LLP in Reston, Va. She received her BA in accounting and her JD from the University of Virginia, holds a CPA from Virginia and is a member of the state bars of Virginia and D.C. She currently lives in Switzerland.

Vera Djordjevich

Vera Djordjevich is a writer and editor in New York. She holds a JD from New York University and a BA in history from Stanford University. A former litigator and legal editor, she is also senior editor of the literary magazine, *On the Page*.

Psst...
Need a Change in Venue?

Use the Internet's most targeted job search tools for law professionals.

Vault Law Job Board
The most comprehensive and convenient job board for law professionals. Target your search by area of law, function, and experience level, and find the job openings that you want. No surfing required.

VaultMatch Resume Database
Vault takes match-making to the next level: post your resume and customize your search by area of law, experience and more. We'll match job listings with your interests and criteria and e-mail them directly to your inbox.

VAULT
> the most trusted name in career information™